Cities for people

Cities for people
Jan Gehl

Washington I Covelo I London

Gehl, Jan, 1936-
Cities for people / Jan Gehl. p. cm.
Includes bibliographical references and index.
ISBN-13: 978-1-59726-573-7 (cloth : alk. paper)
ISBN-10: 1-59726-573-X (cloth : alk. paper)
ISBN-13: 978-1-59726-574-4 (pbk. : alk. paper)
ISBN-10: 1-59726-574-8 (pbk. : alk. paper) 1. City planning.
2. City and town life. 3. City planning--Environmental aspects. I. Title.
HT166.G438 2010
307.1'216--dc22
2010015763

Printed on recycled, acid-free paper ♻

Project team
Birgitte Bundesen Svarre, project manager
Isabel Duckett, design and layout
Camilla Richter-Friis van Deurs, illustrations and cover design
Louise Kielgast, project assistant
Rikke Sode, project assistant
Andrea Have, photo assistant
Karen Ann Steenhard, translation
PJ Schmidt, photo editing

Cover: Waterfront, Casablanca, Morocco, photo, Lars Gemzøe, 2009

This project was made possible with the financial
support of the Realdania Foundation, Copenhagen.

"Above all, do not lose your desire to walk. Every day I walk myself into a state of well-being and walk away from every illness. I have walked myself into my best thoughts, and I know of no thought so burdensome that one cannot walk away from it."

Søren Aabye Kierkegaard
Danish philosopher
1813-1855

Contents

Foreword
by Richard Rogers

Cities are the places where people meet to exchange ideas, trade, or simply relax and enjoy themselves. A city's public domain — its streets, squares, and parks — is the stage and the catalyst for these activities. Jan Gehl, the doyen of public-space design, has a deep understanding of how we use the public domain and offers us the tools we need to improve the design of public spaces and, as a consequence, the quality of our lives in cities.

The compact city — with development grouped around public transport, walking, and cycling — is the only environmentally sustainable form of city. However, for population densities to increase and for walking and cycling to be widespread, a city must increase the quantity and quality of well-planned beautiful public spaces that are human in scale, sustainable, healthy, safe, and lively.

Cities — like books — can be read, and Jan Gehl understands their language. The street, the footpath, the square, and the park are the grammar of the city; they provide the structure that enables cities to come to life, and to encourage and accommodate diverse activities, from the quiet and contemplative to the noisy and busy. A humane city — with carefully designed streets, squares, and parks — creates pleasure for visitors and passers-by, as well as for those who live, work, and play there every day.

Everyone should have the right to easily accessible open spaces, just as they have a right to clean water. Everyone should be able to see a tree from their window, or to sit on a bench close to their home with a play space for children, or to walk to a park within ten minutes. Well-designed neighborhoods inspire the people who live in them, whilst poorly designed cities brutalize their citizens. As Jan says: "We shape cities, and they shape us."

No one has examined the morphology and use of public space to the extent that Jan Gehl has. Anyone who reads this book will get a valuable insight into his astonishingly perceptive understanding of the relationship between public spaces and civic society, and how the two are inextricably intertwined.

London, February 2010
Richard Rogers
Baron Rogers of Riverside
CH, Kt, FRIBA, FCSD

Preface by the author

I graduated as an architect in 1960, which means that I have now been following urban development for 50 years. While there is no doubt that it has been a privilege, the journey has been unsettling as well.

The way cities are planned and developed has dramatically changed character over this span of half a century. Until about 1960 cities throughout the world were primarily developed on the basis of centuries of experience. Life in city space was a vital part of this wealth of experience, and it was taken for granted that cities are built for people.

In step with burgeoning urban growth, city development was turned over to professional planners. Theories and ideologies began replacing tradition as the basis for development. Modernism with its vision of the city as a machine, with its parts separated by function became highly influential. Also a new group, traffic planners, came gradually on the scene with their ideas and theories on how to ensure the best conditions — for car traffic.

Neither the city planners nor the traffic planners put city space and city life high on their agenda, and for years there was hardly any knowledge about how physical structures influence human behavior. The drastic consequences of this type of planning on people's use of the city were not recognized until later.

On the whole city planning over the past 50 years has been problematic. It has not been generally recognized that city life moved from following tradition to becoming a vital city function requiring consideration and careful planning by the professionals.

Now, after many years, a great deal of knowledge has been amassed on the connection between physical form and human behavior. We have extensive information about what can and should be done. At the same time cities and their residents have become very active in crying out for people-oriented city planning. In recent years many cities in all parts of the world have made a serious effort to realize the dream of better cities for people. Many inspiring projects and visionary city strategies point in new directions after years of neglect.

It is now generally accepted that city life and regard for people in city space must have a key role in the planning of cities and built-up areas. Not only has this sector been mismanaged for years, it is also by now realized how caring for people in the city is an important key for achieving more lively, safe, sustainable and healthy cities, all goals of crucial importance in the 21´st century.

It is my hope that this book can make a modest contribution to this important new orientation.

This book was made possible by the close cooperation of a capable and highly motivated team with whom it has been a delight and inspiration to work. I want to extend my heartfelt thanks to Andrea Have and Isabel Duckett for their help with picture editing and graphic layout, to Camilla Richter Friis van Deurs for graphics and illustrations, to Karen Steenhard for the translation of the book from Danish to English, and last but certainly not least to Birgitte Bundesen Svarre, project manager, who steered the author, the team and the project with a steadfast but gentle hand.

My thanks also go to Gehl Architects for providing space and assistance, particularly in the form of many of the illustrations. Thanks to the many friends, research colleagues and photographers from all over the world who generously placed their photographs at our disposal.

I wish to thank Solvejg Reigsted, Jon Pape and Klaus Bech Danielsen for their constructive criticism of content and editing. A very great thanks also goes to Tom Nielsen, Aarhus School of Architecture, for his careful and constructive advice in every phase of the project.

To Lord Richard Rogers, London, my warm thanks for his foreword and valuable introduction to the book.

A profound thanks is further directed to the Realdania Foundation, which provided inspiration for carrying out this project and the financial support to make it possible.

In conclusion a most sincere thanks to my wife, psychologist Ingrid Gehl, who already in the early 1960s pointed my interest to the interaction between form and life as a crucial precondition for good architecture, and who discretely pointed out that this particular area needed much compassion and many studies in the years to come. In all the intervening years Ingrid has provided endless amounts of compassion and insights for both the general cause and for me. Thank you profoundly.

Jan Gehl
Copenhagen, February 2010

XI

1

The human dimension

The human dimension

the human dimension
— overlooked, neglected,
phased out

For decades the human dimension has been an overlooked and haphazardly addressed urban planning topic, while many other issues, such as accomodating the rocketing rise in car traffic, have come more strongly into focus. In addition, dominant planning ideologies — modernism in particular — have specifically put a low priority on public space, pedestrianism and the role of city space as a meeting place for urban dwellers. Finally, market forces and related architectural trends have gradually shifted focus from the interrelations and common spaces of the city to individual buildings, which in the process have become increasingly more isolated, introverted and dismissive.

A common feature of almost all cities — regardless of global location, economic viability and stage of development — is that the people who still use city space in great numbers have been increasingly poorly treated.

Limited space, obstacles, noise, pollution, risk of accident and generally disgraceful conditions are typical for city dwellers in most of the world's cities.

This turn of events has not only reduced the opportunities for pedestrianism as a form of transport, but has also placed the social and cultural functions of city space under siege. The traditional function of city space as a meeting place and social forum for city dwellers has been reduced, threatened or phased out.

a question of life or death
— for five decades

It has been almost 50 years since American journalist and author Jane Jacobs published her seminal book *The Death and Life of Great American Cities* in 1961.[1] She pointed out how the dramatic increase in car traffic and the urban planning ideology of modernism that separates the uses of the city and emphasizes free-standing individual buildings would put an end to urban space and city life and result in lifeless cities devoid of people. She also convincingly described the qualities of living in and enjoying lively cities as seen from her outlook post in Greenwich Village in New York, where she lived.

Jane Jacobs was the first strong voice to call for a decisive shift in the way we build cities. For the first time in the history of man as a settler, cities were no longer being built as conglomerations of city space and buildings, but as individual buildings. At the same time burgeoning car traffic was effectively squeezing the rest of urban life out of urban space.

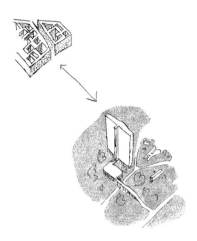

Modernists rejected the city and city space, shifting their focus to individual buildings. This ideology became dominant by 1960, and its principles continue to affect the planning of many new urban areas. If a team of planners was asked to radically reduce life between buildings, they could not find a more effective method than using modernistic planning principles (diagram from Propos d'urbanisme *by Le Corbusier (1946)[2]. Photos from: Täby, Sweden; Melbourne, Australia; and Nuuk, Greenland).*

progress despite the odds

In the five decades since 1961 many researchers and urban planning theoreticians have contributed to the studies and arguments in the discussion of life or death in cities. Much new knowledge has been accumulated.

Valuable progress has also been made in practical urban planning, both in terms of planning principles and traffic planning. Particularly in recent decades, many urban areas around the world have worked hard to create better conditions for pedestrians and city life by making car traffic a lower priority.

Again, primarily in recent decades, there have been a number of interesting departures from modernist urban planning ideals, particularly for new towns and new residential areas. Fortunately, interest in building dynamic, mixed-use urban areas instead of conglomerations of freestanding single buildings is growing.

There has been a corresponding development in traffic planning over the past five decades. Traffic facilities have been made more differentiated,

Cars invaded cities in great numbers all over the world in around 1960, marking the start of a process that eroded the conditions necessary for people to engage in city life. Transgressions were so numerous and so egregious that it is almost impossible to see how detrimental the car invasion has been to city quality (Italy, Ireland and Bangladesh).

principles of traffic calming introduced, and a number of traffic safety steps taken.◀

However, the growth in vehicular traffic has been explosive, and while problems have been addressed in some parts of the world, they have simply grown apace in others.

far greater effort needed

Despite the negative trend of increased automobile use, there have been some positive developments as a reaction to the lack of concern for urban life as found in around 1960.

Not surprisingly, progress and improvements are seen primarily in the most economically advanced parts of the world. In many cases, however, prosperous enclaves have also adopted the ideology of modernism as the starting point for new urban areas and for positioning introverted high-rise buildings in city centers. In these brave new cities, the human dimension has not really been on the agenda, either now or earlier.

In developing countries, the plight of the human dimension is considerably more complex and serious. Most of the population is forced to use city space intensively for many daily activities. Traditionally city space has worked reasonably well for these uses, but when car traffic, for example, grows precipitously, the competition for city space intensifies. The conditions for urban life and pedestrians have become less and less dignified year by year.

the human dimension — a necessary new planning dimension

For the first time in history, shortly after the millennium, the majority of the global population became urban rather than rural. Cities have grown rapidly, and urban growth will continue to accelerate in the years ahead. New and existing cities alike will have to make crucial changes to the assumptions for planning and prioritization. Greater focus on the needs of the people who use cities must be a key goal for the future.

This is the background for the focus on the human dimension of city planning in this book. Cities must urge urban planners and architects to reinforce pedestrianism as an integrated city policy to develop lively, safe, sustainable and healthy cities. It is equally urgent to strengthen the social function of city space as a meeting place that contributes toward the aims of social sustainability and an open and democratic society.

wanted: lively, safe, sustainable and healthy cities

Here at the start of the 21st century, we can glimpse the contours of several new global challenges that underscore the importance of far more targeted concern for the human dimension. Achieving the vision of lively, safe, sustainable and healthy cities has become a general and urgent desire. All four key objectives — lively cities, safety, sustainability, and health — can be strengthened immeasurably by increasing the concern for pedestrians, cyclists and city life in general. A unified citywide political intervention to ensure that the residents of the city are invited to walk and bike as much as possible in connection with their daily activities is a strong reinforcement of the objectives.

a lively city

The potential for a lively city is strengthened when more people are invited to walk, bike and stay in city space. The importance of life in public space, particularly the social and cultural opportunities as well as the attractions associated with a lively city will be discussed in a later section.

a safe city

The potential for a safe city is strengthened generally when more people move about and stay in city space. A city that invites people to walk must by definition have a reasonably cohesive structure that offers short walking distances, attractive public spaces and a variation of urban functions. These elements increase activity and the feeling of security in and around city spaces. There are more eyes along the street and a greater incentive to follow the events going on in the city from surrounding housing and buildings.

a sustainable city

The sustainable city is strengthened generally if a large part of the transport system can take place as "green mobility," that is travel by foot, bike or public transport. These forms of transport provide marked benefits to the economy and the environment, reduce resource consumption, limit emissions, and decrease noise levels.

Another important sustainable aspect is that the attractiveness of public transport systems is boosted if users feel safe and comfortable walking or cycling to and from buses, light rail and trains. Good public space and a good public transport system are simply two sides of the same coin.

a healthy city

The desire for a healthy city is strengthened dramatically if walking or biking can be a natural part of the pattern of daily activities.

We are seeing a rapid growth in public health problems because large segments of the population in many parts of the world have become sedentary, with cars providing door-to-door transport.

A whole-hearted invitation to walk and bike as a natural and integrated element of daily routines must be a nonnegotiable part of a unified health policy.

four goals – one policy

To summarize, increased concern for the human dimension of city planning reflects a distinct and strong demand for better urban quality. There are direct connections between improvements for people in city space and visions for achieving lively, safe, sustainable and healthy cities.[3]

Compared with other social investments — particularly healthcare costs and automobile infrastructure — the cost of including the human dimension is so modest that investments in this area will be possible for cities in all parts of the world regardless of development status and financial capability. In any case, concern and consideration will be the key investment and the benefits enormous.

A lively, safe, sustainable and healthy city is the top-level goal of New York's Plan NYC from 2007.[3] A new bicycle path and widened sidewalk on Broadway in Manhattan (established 2008).[4]

more roads — more traffic. fewer roads — less traffic

After 100 years of car traffic, the notion that more roads lead to more traffic is accepted as fact. In Shanghai, China, and other major cities, more roads do indeed mean more traffic and more congestion.

When the extensive Embarcadero Freeway in San Francisco was closed after the 1989 earthquake, people quickly adapted their traffic behavior and residual traffic found other routes. Today the Embarcadero is a friendly boulevard with trees, trolley cars and good conditions for city life and bicyclists.

In 2002 London introduced road congestion pricing, which meant that motorists have to pay to drive into the designated part of the inner city. From the start, the congestion charge led to a dramatic reduction in vehicular traffic. The fee zone was later expanded towards the west and now comprises almost 50 km²/19 square miles.[5]

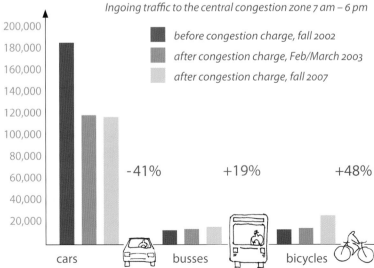

Ingoing traffic to the central congestion zone 7 am – 6 pm

- before congestion charge, fall 2002
- after congestion charge, Feb/March 2003
- after congestion charge, fall 2007

200,000
180,000
160,000
140,000
120,000
100,000
80,000
60,000
40,000
20,000

cars   –41%   busses   +19%   bicycles   +48%

1.2
First we shape the cities — then they shape us

city planning and patterns of use
— a question of invitation

If we look at the history of cities, we can see clearly that urban structures and planning influence human behavior and the ways in which cities operate. The Roman Empire had its colony towns with their fixed and regimented layout of main streets, forums, public buildings and barracks, a formula that reinforced their military role. The compact structure of medieval cities with short walking distances, squares and marketplaces supported their function as centers of trade and craftsmanship. Haussman's strategic urban renewal of Paris in the years after 1852, the broad boulevards in particular, supported military control of the population, as well as providing the platform for a special "boulevard culture" that sprouted promenades and café life along the city's wide streets.

more roads — more traffic

The connection between invitations and behavior came to a head for cities in the 20th century. In the efforts to cope with the rising tide of car traffic, all available city space was simply filled with moving and parked vehicles. Every city got precisely as much traffic as space would allow. In every case, attempts to relieve traffic pressure by building more roads and parking garages have generated more traffic and more congestion. The volume of car traffic almost everywhere is more or less arbitrary, depending on the available transportation infrastructure. Because we can always find new ways to increase our car use, building extra roads is a direct invitation to buy and drive more cars.

fewer roads — less traffic?

If more roads mean more traffic, what happens if fewer cars are invited rather than more? The 1989 earthquake in San Francisco caused so much damage to one of the vital arteries to the city center, the heavily trafficked Embarcadero freeway along the bay, that it had to be closed. Thus a significant traffic route to the city center was removed in one fell swoop, but before plans for reconstruction were off the drawing board, it was clear that the city was managing just fine without it. Users quickly adapted their traffic behavior to the new situation and instead of the damaged double-decker freeway, today there is a city boulevard with trolley cars, trees and wide sidewalks. San Francisco has continued to convert freeways to peaceful city streets in subsequent years. We can find similar examples in Portland, Oregon; Milwaukee, Wisconsin; and Seoul, Korea, where dismantling large road systems reduced capacity and the amount of traffic.

inviting bicyclists: example Copenhagen

Below: going to and from work and education in Copenhagen (2008).

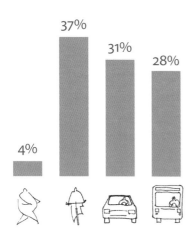

37%

31%

28%

4%

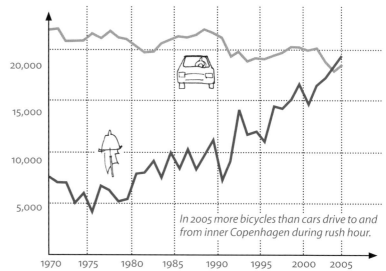

20,000

15,000

10,000

5,000

In 2005 more bicycles than cars drive to and from inner Copenhagen during rush hour.

1970   1975   1980   1985   1990   1995   2000   2005

For many years Copenhagen has invited more bicycle traffic. Networks of good bicycle paths now support a safe and effective alternative transit system. By 2008, bicyclists account for 37% of commutes to and from work and education. The goal is 50%.[6]

The development of a distinct bicycle culture is a significant result of many years of work to invite people to bicycle in Copenhagen. Bicycling has become an important part of the daily activity pattern for all groups of society. More than 50% of Copenhageners bicycle every day.[7]

In 2002 the City of London instituted road pricing for vehicles driving into the city center. The immediate effect of the new "congestion charge" was an 18% traffic reduction in the 24 km² (9.26 sq. miles) central city zone. A few years later traffic increased once again in the area, after which the fee was raised from 5£ to 8£, and traffic has lessened once more. The fee has made the invitation to drive to and from the city a guarded one. Traffic has been reduced, and fees are used to improve public transport systems that by now carry more passengers. The pattern of use has been changed.[8]

better conditions for cyclists — more cyclists

The City of Copenhagen has been restructuring its street network for several decades, removing driving lanes and parking places in a deliberate process to create better and safer conditions for bicycle traffic. Year by year the inhabitants of the city have been invited to bike more. The entire city is now served by an effective and convenient system of bike paths, separated by curbs from sidewalks and driving lanes. City intersections have bicycle crossings painted in blue and, together with special traffic lights for bicycles that turn green six seconds before cars are allowed to move forward, make it considerably safer to cycle around the city. In short a whole-hearted invitation has been extended to cyclists, and the results are reflected clearly in patterns of use.

Bicycle traffic doubled in the period from 1995 to 2005, and in 2008 statistics showed that 37 % of personal transport to and from work and educational institutions was by bicycle. The goal is to increase this percentage considerably in the years to come.[9]

As conditions for bicyclists improve, a new bicycle culture is emerging. Children and seniors, business people and students, parents with young children, mayors and royalty ride bicycles. Bicycling in the city has become the way to get around. It is faster and cheaper than other transport options and also good for the environment and personal health.

An extensive expansion of the opportunities to bicycle in New York began in 2007. Photos show 9th Avenue in Manhattan in April and November 2008 with the new "Copenhagen-style" bicycle path designed so that parked cars protect bicycle traffic. Bicycle traffic has doubled in New York in only two years.

better city space, more city life: example Copenhagen

Average staying acitivites, summer days, noon – 4pm.

1968

1,750

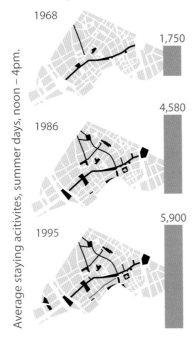

1986

4,580

1995

5,900

A gradual process starting in 1962 has increased car-free areas in Copenhagen. Public spaces public life studies in 1968, 1986 and 1995 show that the extent of staying activities has increased by a factor of four in the period studied. The more space that is offered, the more life comes to the city.[10]
Upper right: Strædet, a Copenhagen street before and after conversion to a pedestrian-priority street in 1992.
Right: Nyhavn converted to a pedestrian street in 1980.

better conditions for city life
— more city life

Not surprisingly, a direct connection between invitations and patterns of use can also be demonstrated for pedestrian traffic and city life.

Many old cities were established as pedestrian cities, and some continue to have that role where topography has made car traffic impossible, or where the economy and social networks are still based on foot traffic.

Venice enjoys an entirely special status among the old pedestrian cities. In its thousand years of history, Venice has functioned continuously as a pedestrian city.

Even today Venice is one of the few cities in the world that is still a pedestrian city because its narrow streets and many canal bridges have prevented cars from gaining access. In the Middle Ages, Venice was the largest and richest city in Europe. This, combined with the fact that for centuries the city was designed and adapted for pedestrian traffic, makes Venice of particular interest today as the model for working with the human dimension.

Venice has everything: dense city structure, short walking distances, beautiful courses of space, high degree of mixed use, active ground floors, distinguished architecture and carefully designed details — and all on a human scale. For centuries Venice has offered a sophisticated framework for city life and continues to do so, issuing a whole-hearted invitation to walk.

Fortunately, we can now study the results of the invitation for increased pedestrianism and city life in cities formerly dominated by car traffic and years of neglect of the human dimension. In recent decades many such cities have made targeted efforts to give pedestrian traffic and city life better conditions.

Developments in Copenhagen, Denmark, and Melbourne, Australia, are of special interest here, because not only have these cities systematically improved the conditions for city life and pedestrian traffic, they have also recorded the development and can document changes and growth in city life in step with the improvements carried out.

Copenhagen
— better city space, more city life

After many years of pruning back pedestrian areas, Copenhagen was one of the first cities in Europe to grasp the nettle in the early 1960s and begin reducing car traffic and parking in the city center in order to create once again better space for city life.

Copenhagen's traditional main street, Strøget, was converted into a pedestrian promenade already in 1962. Skepticism abounded. Would a project like this really succeed so far north?

After only a short period it was clear that the project was enjoying greater success faster than anyone had anticipated. The number of pedestrians rose 35% in the first year alone. It was more comfortable to walk and there was space for more people. Since then, more streets have been converted for pedestrian traffic and city life, and one by one the parking places in the city center have been turned into squares that accommodate public life.

In the period from 1962 to 2005 the area devoted to pedestrians and city life grew by a factor of seven: from approximately 15,000 m² (161,500 sq. feet) to a good 100,000 m² (1,076,000 sq. feet).[11]

Researchers from the School of Architecture, Royal Danish Academy of Fine Arts monitored the development of city life throughout the period. Extensive analyses in 1968, 1986, 1995 and 2005 documented a significant change in city life. The many whole-hearted invitations to walk, stand and sit in the city's common space had resulted in a remarkable new urban pattern: many more people walk and stay in the city.[12]

The pattern in the city center is now being repeated in outlying districts where in recent years many streets and squares have been converted from traffic islands into people-friendly squares. The conclusion from Copenhagen is unequivocal: if people rather than cars are invited into the city, pedestrian traffic and city life increase correspondingly.

better city space, more city life: example Melbourne

Pedestrian traffic in Melbourne

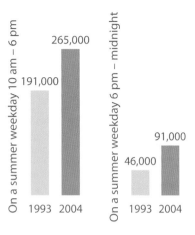

On a summer weekday 10 am – 6 pm

265,000
191,000
1993 2004

On a summer weekday 6 pm – midnight

91,000
46,000
1993 2004

In the years from 1993 to 2004 Melbourne, Australia, carried out an extensive program to improve conditions for life in the city. A study conducted in 2005 showed an increase of pedestrians of 39% from 1993 and three times more people staying for a while in the city. Quality improvements have served as a direct invitation to increased activity in the city.[13]

Federation Square is one of Melbourne's new well-functioning city spaces, and many of the city's neglected lanes and arcades have been incorporated as staying space. All in all, Melbourne has made impressive efforts to invite city dwellers to use their city.

Melbourne — better streets, more squares, more life in the city

In about 1980 Melbourne's inner city was an indifferent collection of offices and high-rises, lifeless and useless. The city was nicknamed "the doughnut" because it was empty in the center. In 1985 an extensive urban renewal project was initiated to transform the city center into a lively and attractive hub for the region's more than three million inhabitants. From 1993 to 1994 the city center's problems were analyzed, the volume of city life documented and an ambitious program of urban improvements drawn up for the next decade.

An impressive number of urban improvements were implemented in the decade from 1994 to 2004. The number of housing units in the city grew by a factor of 10, and the number of inhabitants rose from 1,000 (1992) to almost 10,000 (2002). The number of student enrolments in or near the city center increased by 67%. New squares, including the architecturally significant Federation Square, were laid out, and small arcades, lanes and promenades along the Yarra River were opened up for pedestrian traffic and staying.[15]

The most remarkable factor was, however, the intention to invite people to walk in the city. Since its establishment, Melbourne has been a typical English colony town of broad streets and regular blocks. Early in the urban renewal process, it was decided to pull out the stops to invite people to walk in this city of streets. Sidewalks were expanded, new pavements were laid with local Bluestone, and a system of new city furniture in good materials was designed. The city's pedestrian-friendly profile was followed up by an extensive "green" strategy that included the annual planting of 500 new trees to safeguard the character of and provide shade for the sidewalks. A comprehensive art-in-the-city program and thoughtfully designed night lighting completes the picture of a city that has pursued a targeted policy to invite pedestrian traffic and staying. Two large public spaces public life surveys conducted in

After the conversion of New Road to a pedestrian-priority street in Brighton, England, pedestrian traffic increased by 62%, while the number of staying activities increased by 600%. Photos show New Road before and after conversion in 2006.[14]

The river running through Denmark's second-largest city, Århus, had been covered and used as a major thoroughfare before being reopened in 1998. Since reopening, the recreational pedestrian area along Århus River has been the most popular space in the city. Real estate prices along the river are also among the highest in the city.

1994 and 2004 show that both pedestrian traffic and staying activities have increased markedly in step with the many urban improvements. On the whole, pedestrian traffic during the week in Melbourne's inner city has increased by 39% during the day, while pedestrian use of the city at night has doubled. It is interesting that increase is found not only on individual main streets, but in the city center as a whole. People are flocking to it. Staying activities in the city have also increased dramatically. The new squares, broad sidewalks and newly renovated passages offer many new and attractive staying possibilities, and the activity level has almost tripled on ordinary workdays.[16]

**documenting city life
— an important instrument for city development**

The surveys from Melbourne and Copenhagen are particularly interesting because regular city life surveys have documented that improving conditions for pedestrian traffic and city life lead specifically to new patterns of use and more life in city space. A precise connection between city space quality and the scope of city life has been clearly documented in both Melbourne and Copenhagen — on a city level.

**better city space, more city life
— cities, city space and details**

Not surprisingly, the close connection between people's use of city space, the quality of city space and degree of concern for the human dimension is a general pattern that can be shown at all scales. Just as cities can invite city life, there are many examples of how the renovation of a single space or even change in furniture and details can invite people to a totally new pattern of use.

The river in Århus, Denmark, which was filled in and converted into a street for vehicular traffic in the 1930s, was uncovered in 1996–98 and the spaces along the reopened waterway laid out as recreational pedestrian areas. Since then the areas along the Århus river have been the most commonly used external space in the city. The conversion has been so popular and economically succesfull — the value of the buildings along

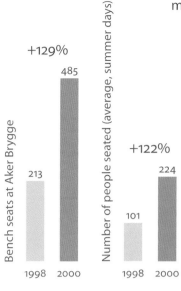

+129%

485

213

Bench seats at Aker Brygge

1998 2000

Number of people seated (average, summer days)

+122%

224

101

1998 2000

More modest invitations can also have a measurable effect. Doubling the number of places to sit in Aker Brygge in Oslo has doubled the number of people who are seated in the area.[17]

the river has more than doubled — that another large section of the river was opened in 2008. The new city space and new invitations have led to completely new patterns of use in the city.

Simple changes such as improvements in bench seating in the harbor of Aker Brygge in Oslo can significantly change the patterns of use. In 1998 the old benches were replaced by new ones that more than doubled the area's seating capacity (+129%). Surveys in 1998 and 2000 before and after the change show that the number of people who sit in the area has correspondingly doubled in response to the new options (+122%).[18]

people in the city
— a question of invitation

The conclusion that if better city space is provided, use will increase is apparently valid in large city public spaces, and individual city spaces and all the way down to the single bench or chair. The conclusion is also generally valid in various cultures and parts of the world, in various climates and in different economies and social situations. Physical planning can greatly influence the pattern of use in individual regions and city areas. Whether people are enticed to walk around and stay in city space is very much a question of working carefully with the human dimension and issuing a tempting invitation.

Every summer the motorway along the Seine River in Paris is closed and converted to "Paris Plage," which is quickly stormed by thousands of Parisians who have been waiting all winter for this very invitation.

necessary, optional and social activities

Necessary activities are an integrated, non optional part of every day. Here we have no choice.

Optional activities are recreational and fun. City quality is a decisive prerequisite for this important group of activities.

Social activities include all types of contact between people and take place everywhere people go in city space.

1.3
The city as meeting place

there is much more to walking than walking!

As a concept, "life between buildings" includes all of the very different activities people engage in when they use common city space: purposeful walks from place to place, promenades, short stops, longer stays, window shopping, conversations and meetings, exercise, dancing, recreation, street trade, children's play, begging and street entertainment.[19]

Walking is the beginning, the starting point. Man was created to walk, and all of life's events large and small develop when we walk among other people. Life in all its diversity unfolds before us when we are on foot.

In lively, safe, sustainable and healthy cities, the prerequisite for city life is good walking oppurtunities. However, the wider perspective is that a multitude of valuable social and recreational opportunities naturally emerge when you reinforce life on foot.

During the many years in which pedestrian traffic was primarily treated as a form of transport that belonged under the auspices of traffic planning, city life's bounty of nuances and opportunities was largely overlooked or ignored. The terms used were "walking traffic," "pedestrian streams," "sidewalk capacity," and "crossing the street safely."

But in cities there is so much more to walking than walking! There is direct contact between people and the surrounding community, fresh air, time outdoors, the free pleasures of life, experiences and information. And at its core walking is a special form of communion between people who share public space as a platform and framework.

it is also — and most particularly about — the city as meeting place

If we take a closer look at the city life studies mentioned earlier, we can see that in city after city where conditions for life on foot are improved, the extent of walking activities increases significantly. We also see even more extensive growth in social and recreational activities.

As mentioned earlier, more roads invite more traffic. Better conditions for bicyclists invite more people to ride bikes, but by improving the conditions for pedestrians, we not only strengthen pedestrian traffic, we also — and most importantly — strengthen city life.

Thus we can elevate the discussion from traffic issues into a far broader, more wide-ranging and important discussion concerning living conditions and human options in the city.

multifacetted city life

A common characteristic of life in city space is the versatility and complexity of the activities, with much overlapping and frequent shifts be-

tween purposeful walking, stopping, resting, staying and conversing. Unpredictability and unplanned, spontaneous actions are very much part of what makes moving and staying in city space such a special attraction. We are on our way, watching people and events, inspired to stop to look more closely or even to stay or join in.

necessary activities
— under all conditions

A clear core pattern emerges from the great diversity of activities in city space. One simple way to look at them is to put the most important categories on a scale according to their degree of necessity. At one end of the scale are the purposeful necessary activities, that is, activities that people generally have to undertake: going to work or school, waiting for the bus, bringing goods to customers. These activities take place under all conditions.[1]

optional activities
— under good conditions

At the other end of this scale are the largely recreational, optional activities that people might like: walking down the promenade, standing up to get a good look at the city, sitting down to enjoy the view or the good weather.[1]

The great majority of the most attractive and popular city activities belong to this group of optional activities, for which good city quality is a prerequisite.

If outdoor conditions make walking and recreating impossible, such as during a snowstorm, just about nothing happens. If conditions are tolerable, the extent of necessary activities grows. If conditions for being outdoors are good, people engage in many necessary activities and also an increasing number of optional ones. Walkers are tempted to stop to enjoy the weather, places and life in the city, or people emerge from their buildings to stay in city space. Chairs are dragged out in front of houses, and children come out to play.

versatile city life depends largely on invitation

For good reason, climate is mentioned as an important factor for the extent and character of outdoor activities. If it is too cold, too hot or too wet, outdoor activities are reduced or rendered impossible.

Another very important factor is the physical quality of city space. Planning and design can be used to influence the extent and character of outdoor activities. Invitations to do something outdoors other than just walking should include protection, security, reasonable space, furniture and visual quality.

The city life studies mentioned also document the great opportunities for actively inviting people not only to walk but to participate in a versatile and varied city life.

diverse city life – as an old tradition and contemporary city policy

Cities and urban areas can set the stage for specific activities. In the inner city streets of Tokyo, London, Sydney and New York people walk: there isn't room for anything else. In vacation and tourist areas, where passing the time, consumption and pleasure are top priorities, people are invited to stroll and stay a while. In traditional cities such as Venice, people are invited to a versatile and complex city life where there are good conditions for both pedestrian traffic and staying. Corresponding patterns of activity can be found in Copenhagen, Lyon, Melbourne and in other cities, large and small, that have significantly improved conditions for life in city space in recent decades. Pedestrian traffic has grown, and the number of recreational, optional activities has swelled.

interplay between city life and the quality of city space. Example: New York

Although pedestrian traffic has traditionally dominated the streets of Manhattan in New York City, in 2007 an extensive program was launched to encourage greater versatility in city life.[20] The idea was to provide better options for recreation and leisure as a supplement to the extensive purposeful pedestrian traffic. For example, on Broadway expanded

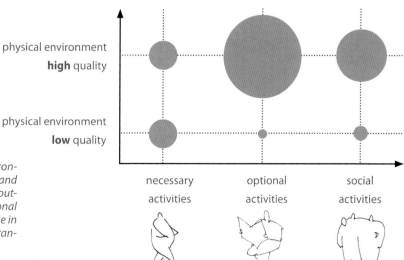

Graphic representation of the connection between outdoor quality and outdoor activities. An increase in outdoor quality gives a boost to optional activities in particular. The increase in activity level then invites a substantial increase in social activities.

In 2009 Broadway in New York City was closed to traffic at Times Square and Herald Square, which brought quiet, dignity and 7,000 more square meters/75,000 square feet to city life. The activity level in the new spaces has been impressive from day one.[21] Left: Times Square before and right after the redesign.

sidewalks have provided room for café chairs and places to stay, while a number of new car-free areas with many opportunities to stay have been established at Madison Square, Herald Square and Times Square. In all these cases the new opportunities were adopted at once. Almost day-by-day the new invitations have enriched city life and made it far more multifaceted. Even in New York City there is obviously a need for city space and great interest in participating more in city life now that there are more opportunities and solid invitations.

necessary and optional activities as prerequisite for social city activities

That both the character and the extent of city life are influenced dramatically by the quality of city space is in itself an important connection. The connection becomes even more interesting if we look at the relationships between necessary, optional and the important group of social activities. If city life is reinforced, it creates the preconditions for strengthening all forms of social activity in city space.

social activities
— the city as meeting place

Social activities include all types of communication between people in city space and require the presence of other people. If there is life and activity in city space, there are also many social exchanges. If city space is desolate and empty, nothing happens.

Social activities include a wide spectrum of diverse activities. There are many passive see and hear contacts: watching people and what is happening. This modest, unpretentious form of contact is the most widespread social city activity anywhere.

There are more active contacts. People exchange greetings and talk to acquaintances they meet. There are chance meetings and small talk at market booths, on benches and wherever people wait. People ask for directions and exchange brief remarks about the weather or when the next bus is due. More extensive contact can sometimes grow from these short greetings. New topics and common interests can be discussed. Acquaintanceships can sprout. Unpredictability and spontaneity are key words. Among the more extensive contacts are children's play or the young people who "hang out" and use city space as a meeting place.

Finally, there is a large group of more or less planned common activities: markets, street parties, meetings, parades and demonstrations.

much to look at and important information

As mentioned earlier, see and hear activities are the largest category of social contact. This is also the form of contact that can most directly be influenced by urban planning. Invitations largely determine whether city spaces have the life that gives people the opportunity to meet. The issue is important because these passive see and hear contacts provide the background and springboard for the other forms of contact. By watching, listening and experiencing others, we gather information about people and the society around us. It is a start.

Experiencing life in the city is also diverting and stimulating entertainment. The scene changes by the minute. There is much to see: behavior, faces, colors and feelings. And these experiences are related to one of the most important themes in human life: people.

"man is man's greatest joy"

The statement that "man is man's greatest joy" comes from Hávamál, a more than 1,000-year-old Icelandic Eddic poem, which succinctly describes human delight and interest in other people. Nothing is more important or more compelling.[22]

Even from their cradles babies strain to see as much as possible, and later they crawl all over their homes to follow the action. Older children bring their toys into the living room or kitchen to be where the action is. Outside play takes place not necessarily on playgrounds or in traffic-free areas, but more often on the street, in parking lots or in front of entrance doors, where the grown-ups are. Young people hang out by entrances and on street corners to follow along with — and perhaps join in — events.

All over the world, guests at sidewalk cafés turn toward the number one city attraction: city life (Strasbourg, France).

"man is man's greatest joy"

Girls look at boys and vice versa — throughout their lives. Older people follow the life and activities of the neighborhood from their windows, balconies and benches.

Throughout life we have a constant need for new information about people, about life as it unfolds and about the surrounding society. New information is gathered wherever people are and therefore very much in common city space.

the city's greatest attraction: people

Studies from cities all over the world illuminate the importance of life and activity as an urban attraction. People gather where things are happening and spontaneously seek the presence of other people.

Faced with the choice walking down a deserted or a lively street, most people would choose the street with life and activity. The walk will be more interesting and feel safer. Studies from inner-city shopping streets in Copenhagen show how happenings, events and building sites where we can watch people perform, play music or build houses attract far more people to linger and watch than shops along building façades. Studies of benches and chairs in city space show correspondingly that the seats with the best view of city life are used far more frequently that those that do not offer a view of other people.[23]

The placement and use of café chairs tells a similar story. The most important attraction of a sidewalk café has always been the sidewalk and thus the view of life in the city, and the majority of café chairs are placed accordingly.

delight in life in the city
— in perspective drawings

Nothing speaks greater volumes about "life between buildings" as an attraction than the architect's perspective drawings. Regardless of whether the human dimension is carefully treated or totally neglected in the projects, the drawings are full of cheerful, happy people. The many people depicted in the drawings give projects an aura of happiness and attractiveness, sending the signal that good human qualities are in abundance, whether or not this is the case. That people are people's greatest delight is obvious — at least in the drawings!

the city as meeting place
— in an historic perspective

Throughout history city space has functioned as a meeting place on many levels for city dwellers. People met, exchanged news, made deals, arranged marriages — street artists entertained and goods were offered for sale. People attended city events large and small. Processions were held, power was manifested, parties and punishments held publicly — everything was carried out in full public view. The city was the meeting place.

under pressure from the car
invasion and modernistic
planning ideology

City space continued to function as an important social meeting place in the 20th century, until the planning ideals of modernism prevailed and coincided with the car invasion. The discussion of "death and life" in cities, raised defiantly by Jane Jacob's book in 1961, dealt in large part with the gradual breakdown of the opportunities of city space to function as a meeting place.[24] Even though the discussion has continued since then, city life has in many places continued to be squeezed out of city space.

Dominant planning ideologies have rejected city space and city life as untimely and unnecessary. Planning has been heavily dedicated to the ideal of developing a rational and streamlined setting for necessary activities. Increasing car traffic has swept city life off the stage or made travel by foot totally impossible. Trade and service functions have largely been concentrated in large indoor shopping malls.

the neglected cities — and city life cancelled!

We can see the results of these trends in many cities, particularly in the southern USA. In many cases people have abandoned cities and it is largely impossible to get to the various facilities in the city without a car. Pedestrianism, city life and the city as meeting place have all been cancelled.

the city as meeting place — in the 21st century

Access to indirect information and contacts has grown explosively in recent years. The TV, internet, e-mail and mobile telephone give us extensive and easily accessible contact to people all over the world. From time to time the question arises: can the function of city space as meeting place now be taken over by the host of electronic options?

The development of life in cities in recent years suggests a completely different picture. Here the indirect contacts and stream of images depicting what others have experienced in other places does not out compete life in public spaces, but rather stimulates people to join in and play an active personal role. Opportunities to be there in person, face-to-face meetings and the surprising and unpredictable character of experiences are qualities tied to city space as meeting place.

Towns devoid of people are a widespread phenomenon in the southern United States. Pedestrians and city life have given up and everything must be done by car (Clarksdale, Mississippi).

New indirect forms of communication are on the march. They can supplement but not replace direct meetings between people.

It is interesting to note that in these very same decades in which city life has undergone a remarkable renaissance, electronic means of contact have been introduced. We need both options.

Many social changes, particularly in the wealthiest parts of the world, can explain the increased interest in getting about and staying in the city's common space. Longevity, plentiful free time and better economy in general have left more time and more resources for recreation and pleasure.

By 2009, half of Copenhagen's households were inhabited by only one person.[25] Shrinking households increase the need for social contacts outside the home. As a result of the numerous changes in the way society and the economy are organized, many people now live an in-

Walking in the city invites direct experiences for all senses as well as attractive extra opportunities to exchange smiles and glances (Robson Street, Vancouver, Canada).

Public space has significant social importance as a forum for the exchange of ideas and opinions.

creasingly more privatized life with private residence, private car, private household machines and private offices. In this situation we see steadily growing interest in strengthening contacts to the civil society at large.

These new opportunities and needs can largely explain the dramatic increase in the use of the city's common space that is evident in all the cities that have worked in recent years with reviving invitations to city life.

city as meeting place
— in a societal perspective

To a far greater extent than private commercial arenas, public democratically managed city space provides access and opportunities for all groups of society to express themselves and latitude for non-mainstream activities.

The spectrum of activities and actors demonstrates the opportunities for public city space generally to strengthen social sustainability. It is a significant quality that all groups of society, regardless of age, income, status, religion or ethnic background, can meet face to face in city space as they go about their daily business. This is a good way to provide general information to everyone about the composition and universality of society. It also makes people feel more secure and confident about experiencing the common human values played out in many different contexts.

Newspapers and TV represent the opposite of this obvious opportunity for people to experience firsthand the daily life of the city. The information these media communicate focuses mainly on reports of accidents and attacks, and presents a distorted picture of what actually goes on in society. Fear and gross generalizations abound in this kind of atmosphere.

It is interesting to note that crime prevention strategies emphasize strengthening common space so that meeting people from various groups of society is a routine part of everyday life. We can think of closeness, trust and mutual consideration as the direct opposites of walls, gates and more police presence on the street.

the democratic dimension

Public interests determine the playing rules in the common space of the city and thus help to ensure people's opportunities to exchange personal, cultural and political messages.

The importance of city space is underlined in the First Amendment to the Constitution of the United States, which sets out freedom of speech and the right of assembly for its citizens. This importance is also underscored by the frequent bans on assembly in city space decreed by totalitarian regimes.

As an open and accessible interface between people, city space provides an important arena for large political meetings, demonstrations and protests, as well as for more modest activities such as collecting signatures, handing out flyers or staging happenings or protests.

the city as meeting place
— small events and large perspectives

Social sustainability, security, confidence, democracy and freedom of speech are key concepts for describing societal perspectives tied to the city as meeting place.

Life in city space is all-encompassing: from momentary glances to minor events to the largest collective manifestations. Walking through common city space can be a goal in itself – but also a beginning.

cities by people and for people

Unlike the city space of Venice, the reconquered city space in Copenhagen, Melbourne and New York does not represent a nostalgic traditional idyll. These are contemporary cities with solid economies, large populations and versatile city functions. What is remarkable about them is that they reflect a growing understanding that cities must be designed to invite pedestrian traffic and city life. These cities recognize the importance of pedestrian traffic and bicyclists for sustainability and health in society, and they acknowledge the importance of city life as an attractive, informal and democratic meeting place for their residents in the 21st century.

❜ After almost 50 years of neglect of the human dimension, here at the beginning of the 21st century we have an urgent need and growing willingness to once again create cities for people.❜

2

Senses and scale

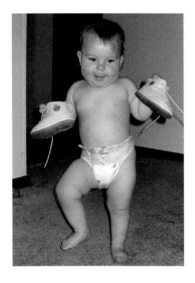

The client: a linear, frontal, horizontal, maximum 5 km/h – 3 mph human being (Laura, age 1).

The basic elements of city architecture are movement space and experience space. The street reflects the linear movement pattern of feet and the square represents the area the eye can take in (Stone Town, Zanzibar, Tanzania, and Ascoli Piceno, Italy).

This little town is nestled in the bay like a corner sofa in the living room. Its back is covered and the scenery is on a human scale. This is a good place to be — also for a town (Portofino, Italy).

Senses and scale

a linear, frontal, horizontal mammal walking at max 5 km/h – 3 mph

The natural starting point for the work of designing cities for people is human mobility and the human senses because they provide the biological basis for activities, behavior and communication in city space.

Twenty-first century urban pedestrians are the result of an evolution over millions of years. Man has evolved to move slowly and on foot, and the human body is linear in orientation.

While our feet can walk or run forward with ease, they move backwards or sideways with great difficulty. Our senses have also developed to allow slow, forward movement on largely horizontal surfaces.

Our eyes, ears and nose face forward to help us sense danger and opportunities on the route ahead. The rods and cones in the photoreceptor layer of the eye are organized to match our horizontal, earth-bound field of experience.

We can see clearly ahead, peripherally to the sides, downward to some extent and much less upwards. Our arms also point forward and are well positioned for touching something or pushing branches aside along our route. In short, Homo sapiens are a linear, frontal, horizontally oriented upright mammal. Paths, streets and boulevards are all spaces for linear movement designed on the basis of the human locomotor system.

One of the most memorable moments in life is the day a child stands upright and starts walking: now life is about to start in earnest.

So here is our client, a pedestrian with all his attributes, potential and limitations. Basically, working with the human scale means providing good city spaces for pedestrians that take into account the possibilities and limitations dictated by the human body.

distance and perception

In his books *The Silent Language* (1959) and *The Hidden Dimension* (1966), the American anthropologist Edward T. Hall has provided an excellent survey of human evolutionary history and an introduction to human senses, their features and importance.[1]

Sensory development is closely tied to evolutionary history and can be simply classified into the "distance" senses: seeing, hearing and smelling, and the "close" senses: feeling and tasting, which are related to the skin and muscles and thus the ability to feel cold, heat and pain as well as texture and shape. In contact between people, the senses come into play at highly disparate distances.

Sight is the most highly developed of our senses. First we register an-

100 m / 328 ft
80 m / 262 ft
50 m / 164 ft
20 m / 66 ft
10 m / 33 ft
7.5 m / 25 ft
5 m / 16.5 ft
2 m / 6.5 ft
0.5 m / 1.6 ft

We can see people 100 meters/328 feet away, and if the distance is shortened, we can see a bit more. But the experience only becomes interesting and exciting at a distance of less than 10 meters/33 feet, and preferably at even closer ranges where we can use all our senses.[2]

other human being as a dim shape in the distance. Depending on the background and light, we can identify people as human rather than animals or bushes at a distance of 300 to 500 meters (330 to 550 yards).

Only when the distance has been reduced to about 100 meters (110 yards) can we see movement and body language in broad outline. Gender and age can be identified as the pedestrian approaches, and we usually recognize the person at somewhere between 50 and 70 meters (55 and 75 yards). Hair color and characteristic body language can also be read from this distance.

At a distance of about 22 – 25 meters (24 – 27 yards), we can accurately read facial expression and dominant emotions. Is the person happy, sad, excited or angry? Increasingly more detail becomes visible as the person comes closer, with the viewer's field of vision being directed to the upper body, then to the face only and finally only to parts of the face. In the meantime, the person has long been within hearing distance: At 50 – 70 meters (55 – 75 yards) we can hear shouts for help. At 35 meters (38 yards) one-way communication can be conducted in a loud voice like that used from the pulpit, stage or auditorium. At a distance of 20 to 25 meters (22 to 27 yards), short messages can be exchanged, but genuine conversation is not possible until people are within seven meters (7.5 yards) of each other. The shorter the distance in the range from seven meters (7.5 yards) to half a meter (19.5 inches), the more detailed and articulated the conversation can be.[3]

The other senses also come into play as distance lessens: we can smell sweat or perfume. We can sense temperature differences on the skin, an important means of communication. Blushing, affectionate glances and white-hot anger are exchanged close up. Physical affection and touching are naturally also relegated to this intimate sphere.

social field of vision

We can summarize these observations about distance, senses and communication by saying that very little happens at distances from 100 to about 25 meters (110 to 27 yards), after which richness of detail and communication intensify dramatically meter by meter (yard by yard). Finally, between seven to zero meters (7.5 to 0 yards), all of the senses can be used, all details experienced and the most intense feelings exchanged.

In an urban planning context, where the relationship between the senses, communication and dimensions is an important theme, we speak of a social field of vision. The limit of this field is 100 meters (110 yards), the point at which we can see people in motion.

Twenty-five meters (27 yards) is another significant threshold, the one at which we can start decoding emotions and facial expressions. Not surprisingly, these two distances are key in many physical settings where the focus is on watching people.[4]

watching events

Arenas built for spectator events such as concerts, parades and sports bring the 100-meter (110-yard) distance into play once more. For athletics or sports matches where spectators need to keep their eye not only on the overall situation but also on the ball, people and movement, the distance from mid-field to the furthest seats is about 100 meters (110 yards).

Arenas are designed so that the seating towers above the field itself. That way spectators see everything slightly from above, which is usually not a problem for sports events, where the general patterns of activity are themselves an important part of the attraction. Tickets can be sold as long as seats are located within the magic range of approximately 100 meters (110 yards) — the distance from which we can see people moving.

This 100-meter (110-yard) distance also provides an upper limit to how many people can be packed together. Even the largest arenas can only accommodate a relatively limited number of spectators with a maximum of about 100,000 seats, such as Barcelona's football arena Camp Nou (98,772) or the Olympic Stadium in Beijing (91,000).

to see events

The ability to see people at distances up to 100 meters/328 feet is reflected in the dimensions of spectator space for watching sports and other events.

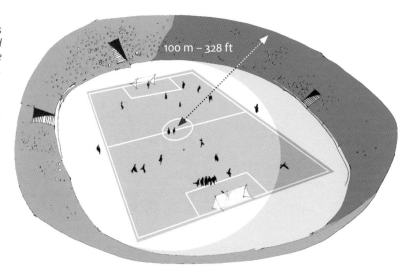

100 m – 328 ft

What we have here is a highly effective 100-meter (110-yard) "viewing wall," a biological limit to the size of such facilities. If the number of spectators is to be increased, the focus of their viewing attention must be magnified. At rock concerts both picture and sound are magnified on a large screen adapted to the total size of the spectator space. At drive-in theatres movies are projected onto a giant screen so that viewers can follow the action even from quite a distance.

experiencing emotion

The second threshold value appears in the theatre or opera house, namely the approximately 25 meters (27 yards) from which facial expression, well-articulated singing and conversation can be experienced. In both the theater and the opera, the primary purpose of communication is to evoke mood and emotion. Faces must be visible and variations in vocal pitch heard.

If we look at theatres and opera houses around the world, however, the critical distance between stage and the most distant seats turns out to be 35 rather than 25 meters (38/27 yards). The reason for this enlarged spectator extension can be found in the actors' body language, make-up and voice projection. Make-up accentuates and exaggerates facial expression, body movements are cleverly emphasized, body language becomes "theatrical," and language is modulated through articulation and exaggeration, as is known from the "stage whisper" that can be heard 35 meters (38 yards) away. All these ploys give theatergoers a strong impression of the emotions being played out — even though the stage is actually 35 meters (38 yards) away. That is the limit of what is possible.

Theaters and opera houses also extend the seating in height and to the sides in order to achieve the greatest capacity. Ground-floor orchestra seating is supplemented by one, two or even three balconies that tower above the stage, as well as side balconies raised high above the stage floor. The magic 35 meters (38 yards) is the common denominator that allows us to sense and feel.

When emotion rather than motion is in the spotlight, 35 m / 115 feet is the magic number. Used in theatres and opera houses all over the world, this is the greatest distance at which audiences can read facial expression and hear speech and song.

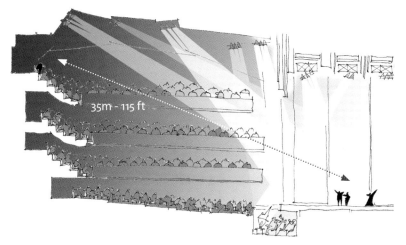

35m - 115 ft

you get the experience you pay for

Even though a space can physically accommodate a certain number of spectators, the quality of the experience varies dramatically, and this difference is reflected equally dramatically in ticket prices. The highest prices are exacted for seats in the middle of the theatre closest to the stage, in the first rows on the ground floor or first rows in the balcony. From these seats the audience can view the performance frontally, up close and more or less at eye level. The most powerful experience is to be had here. Seats cost less further back because the experience is less intense, although it is still frontal and at eye level. Higher up, further away and further out to the sides, the experience becomes more distant and the view more awkward, and ticket prices are correspondingly lower. Finally there are the cheapest seats in the uppermost balcony and all the way out to the sides. In fact from these seats you can't really see the performance, only the actors' wigs and the patterns in which they move. In compensation these ticket-holders can hear the actors' lines and get a good view of the wings.

Theatre seats and ticket prices tell us something significant about our sensory apparatus and human communication. Key words for the most attractive seating are: close up, largely frontal and at the same level. Key

Our sense of sight has developed to enable us to see and comprehend what is happening on the horizontal plane. If we see people and events from above or below, it is rather difficult for us to grasp essential information.

words for the less attractive seating are: greater distance and seen from the side. Least attractive by far is the view from on high. From this perspective the viewer can see distant views, but certainly not faces and emotions.

scale, senses and the dimensions of city space

The social field of vision at approximately 100 meters (110 yards) is also reflected in the size of most squares and plazas in old cities. The 100-meter (110-yard) distances enables onlookers to stand on one corner and get a general view of what is going on in the square. Walk a few paces into the square and at 60 – 70 meters (65 – 77 yards) they can begin to recognize people and thus see who else is there.

Many old squares in Europe are found within this range of dimensions. Squares are rarely larger than 10,000 m² (11,960 sq. yards), with the majority measuring 6 – 8,000 m² (7,000 – 9,500 sq. yards), and many are much smaller. If we look at dimensions, distances greater than 100 meters (110 yards) are rare and 80–90-meter (87–98-yard) lengths much more common. Width varies from plazas that are geometrically square to those that have the more common rectangular shape, and a typical measurement may be 100 x 70 meters (110 x 76 yards). In a square of this size you can see activities everywhere. If you take a walk through the square, you can see most faces within the 25 meters (27 yards) that enable you to observe facial expression and detail. The dimensions of the space offer the best of two worlds: overview and detail.

In the Tuscan town of Siena, the main square, Piazza del Campo, is a large space. It is longest on the Town Hall side, 135 meters (147 yards), and 90 meters (98 yards) on the other dimension. A row of bollards just inside the perimeter creates a new space at about the magic 100 meters (110 yards) distance of experience. The middle of the square, which is sunken like a deep bowl, provides a perfect view and a space for activities. The Campo in Siena demonstrates that large spaces can also have a human dimension, provided they are carefully designed.

the square — staying and activity space proportioned to match the eye's ability

Where paths and streets were described in the preceding section as movement space whose form can be directly related to the linear movement of feet, squares and plazas as spatial shape can correspondingly be related to the eye and its potential to grasp events within a radius of 100 meters (110 yards).Whereas the street signals movement: "please move on," psychologically the square signals staying. Whereas movement space says "go, go, go," the square says: "stop and see what's happening here." Both feet and eyes have left an indelible mark on urban planning history. The basic building blocks of urban architecture are movement space: the street, and experience space: the square.

a horizontal sensory apparatus

It has already been mentioned that the price of theatre tickets falls dramatically when the performance cannot be experienced at eye level —

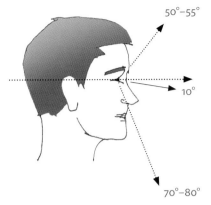

50°–55°

10°

70°–80°

Our sense of sight has developed to enable us to walk on a horizontal plane. We do not see much above us and only slightly more when we look down in order to avoid obstacles in our path. In addition, we typically bow our heads 10 degrees while we are walking.[5]

Low buildings are in keeping with the human horizontal sensory apparatus, but high buildings are not (Bo01 and Turning Torso, Malmø, Sweden).

The location of the vegetables in front of the shop makes its own statement about field of vision.

with the view from the highest balcony being particularly unpopular. The explanation is mankind's horizontally developed sensory apparatus. As they evolved, sight, the other senses and the body have adapted to a situation in which their owners moved linearly and horizontally at a walking pace. Earlier in our history it was important for walkers to be able to detect dangers and enemies lurking ahead, and to spot thorns and scorpions on the path in front of them. It was also crucial to be able to keep an eye on what was happening on both sides of the path.

The eye can see clearly and precisely straight ahead and at a great distance. Furthermore, the rods and cones in the photoreceptor layer of the eye are organized primarily horizontally, enabling us to see movement further out in the field of vision, perpendicular to the walking direction.

However, our downward and upward sight has developed very differently. Looking down where it is important to see what we are stepping on,

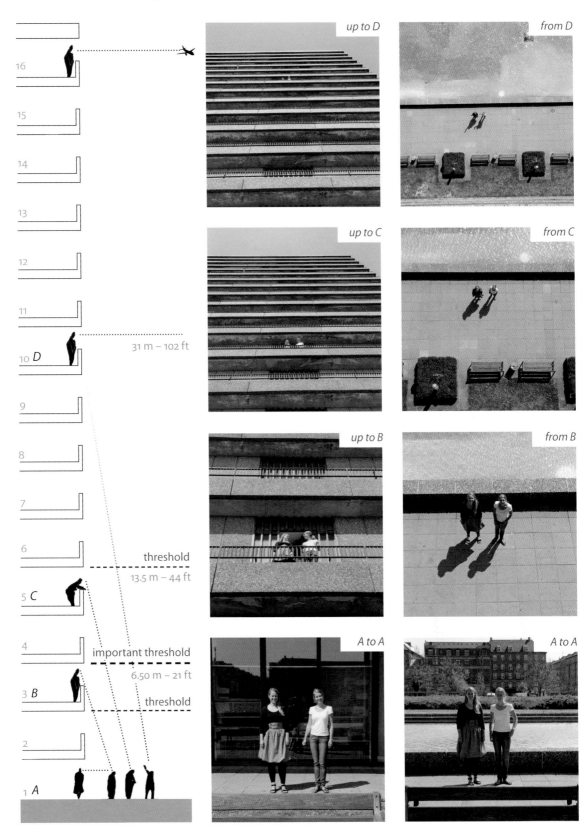

up to D

from D

up to C

from C

31 m – 102 ft

up to B

from B

threshold
13.5 m – 44 ft

important threshold

6.50 m – 21 ft

threshold

A to A

A to A

Left: contact between building and street is possible from the lowest five floors. Contact with the city quickly dissipates above the fifth floor, with the contact interface changing to views, clouds and airplanes.

we humans can see up to 70 – 80 degrees below the horizon. Upwards, where in the later phases of evolutionary history we had only few enemies to beware of, the angle of vision is limited to 50 – 55 degrees above the horizon.

In addition, we can move our head quickly from side to side if we need to focus on something happening by the roadside. It is also easy to bend our head down, and in fact our head is usually inclined about 10 degrees downward during normal walking so that we can better assess the situation on the path. Raising our head upward is much more difficult.[6]

Our senses and our locomotor apparatus paint a clear picture of an extremely alert pedestrian who looks ahead and down, but has only a limited field of upward vision. Thus hiding in trees has always been a good idea. Looking down is easy enough, but looking up is another story: we have to literally "crane our necks."

This whole account of the horizontal sensory apparatus is the key to how we experience space, for example, how much of buildings pedestrians experience when walking along streets. Naturally that also impacts on the experience of low-rise and tall buildings in cities. In general, the upper floors of tall buildings can only be seen at a distance and never close up in the cityscape.

Events that take place in urban space or in the doors and windows on ground floors can be seen at a distance of up to 100 meters (110 yards). In these situations, we can also get close up and bring all our senses to bear. From the street, we can only experience with difficulty events that take place higher up in buildings. The higher up, the more difficult it is to see. We have to move further and further back to look up, distances become greater and greater, and what we see and experience dimin-

Our horizontal field of visions means that when we are walking along building façades, only the ground floors can offer us interest and intensity. If ground floor façades are rich in variation and detail, our city walks will be equally rich in experience (street in Gamla Stan, Stockholm, Sweden, and ground floors in Dublin, Ireland).

When we walk we have time to see faces and details (Piazza Navona, Rome, Italy). And it is still possible to see a fair amount of detail when we bicycle (18 km/h – 11 mph) or run (12 km/h – 7.5 mph).

ishes. Shouting and gesticulating don't help much. In fact the connection between street plane and tall buildings is effectively lost after the fifth floor.[7]

Communication from tall buildings to their surroundings is correspondingly excellent from the two lower stories and feasible from the third, fourth and fifth floors. From there we can watch and follow the life of the city; talking, shouting and arm movements can be perceived. We are actually taking part in the life of the city. Above five stories the situation changes drastically. Details cannot be seen, people on the ground can neither be recognized nor contacted. Above the fifth floor, offices and housing should logically be the province of the air-traffic authorities. At any rate, they no longer belong to the city.

perception and speed
— a 5 km/h (3 mph) creature
that can also manage 15 km/h (9
mph)

Our sensory apparatus and systems for interpreting sensory impressions are adapted to walking. When we walk at our usual speed of four to five km/h (2.5 – 3 mph), we have time to see what is happening in front of us and where to place our feet on the path ahead. If we meet other people, we can see them from a distance of 100 meters (110 yards). It takes between 60 and 70 seconds before we actually meet face to face. Within this timeframe our volume of perceived information increases, and there is plenty of time to assess and respond to the situation.

When running at 10 – 12 km/h (6 – 7 mph), we can still perceive and process sensory impressions and thus gain an acceptable level of control over the situation, assuming that the road is even and the surroundings reasonably easy to comprehend. It is interesting that the running experience largely corresponds to cycling at an ordinary speed of 15 – 20 km/h (9 – 12 mph). As cyclists we are also in good sensory contact with our surroundings and other people.[8]

If the road is full of obstacles or the big picture is too complex, our running and cycling speed drop because otherwise we wouldn't have time to see, understand and react. We have to slow down to about five km/t (three mph) to grasp the overall picture as well as the details.

Motorway accidents are a good example of how important low speed is to our having enough time to see what has happened, with drivers in the opposite lanes typically braking and crawling past at walking speed to watch. Another and far less macabre example is the lecturer who shows his slides too quickly, until the audience asks for more time to look at each one.

human scale — and car scale

At speeds greater than walking or running, our chances of seeing and understanding what we see are greatly diminished. In old cities where traffic was based on walking pace, space and buildings were designed as a matter of course on a five km/h (three mph) scale. Pedestrians don't

5 km/h (3 mph) architecture and 60 km/h (36 mph) architecture.

5 km/h (3 mph) architecture — 60 km/h (37 mph) architecture

5 km/h (3 mph)

60 km/h (37 mph)

5 km/h (3 mph)

60 km/h (37 mph)

The 5 km/h (3 mph) scale has small spaces, small signals, many details — and people close by. The 60 km/h (37 mph) scale has large spaces, large signals and no details. At that speed it is not possible to see details — or people.

take up much space and can easily maneuver in a narrow setting. They have time and leisure to study the details of buildings up close as well as survey mountains in the distance. People can similarly be experienced both at a distance and right close up.

Five km/h (three mph) architecture is based on a cornucopia of sensory impressions, spaces are small, buildings are close together and the combination of detail, faces and activities contributes to the rich and intense sensory experience.

Driving in a car at 50, 80 or 100 km/h (31, 50 or 62 mph), we miss out on the opportunity to grasp detail and see people. At such high speeds spaces need to be large and readily manageable, and all signals have to be simplified and magnified so that drivers and passengers can take in the information.

The 60 km/h (37 mph) scale has large spaces and wide roads. Buildings are seen at a distance, and only generalities are perceived. Details and multifaceted sensory experiences disappear, and from the perspective of a pedestrian, all signs and other information are grotesquely magnified.

Taking a walk in 60 km/h (37 mph) architecture is an impoverished sensory experience: uninteresting and tiring.

Venice is a 5 km/h (3 mph) city with small spaces, elegant signals, fine details and many people. It is a city that offers a wealth of experiences and sensory impressions.

Dubai is primarily a 100 km/h (62 mph) city: large spaces, large signals, large buildings and high noise level.

0 – 45 cm (0 – 18 in.):
intimate distance.

45 – 120 cm (18 in. to 4 ft):
personal distance.

1.2 – 3.7 m (4 – 12 ft):
social distance.

Above 3.7 m (12 ft):
public distance.

large distances: many impressions, short distances: strong impressions

We gather large volumes of information over great distances, while we take in few but very intense and emotionally significant sensory impressions from short distances. What is common to the senses that function at short distance — smell and touch and thus also the ability to capture temperature signals — is that they are the senses most closely tied to our emotions.

In communication between people there are very few changes in the range between 10 and 100 meters (11 and 110 yards), while at short distances, the nature of contact changes dramatically almost centimeter by centimeter (inch by inch). Warm, personal and intense communication takes place at very short distances.[9]

four communication distances

Different forms of communication take place at different distances, and distances vary constantly depending on the subject and nature of the contact. Studies of communication distances have pinpointed four important thresholds for communication. For example, as Edward T. Hall described in *The Hidden Dimension*, four distinct communication distances can be defined through changes in voice levels in particular.[10]

When spectators want to stand at a comfortable public distance from street artists, the result is a circle with good space in the middle for the entertainment (Pompidou Center, Paris, France).

Intimate distance — 0 to 45 cm (0 to 18 in.) — is the distance at which strong emotions can be exchanged. This is the distance of love, tenderness and consolation, as well as the distance for communicating anger and rage. At this distance the senses most closely tied to our feelings, smell and touch, are in play. We can hug, pat, feel and touch. Contact is close, warm, intense and emotionally charged.

Personal distance — 45 cm to 1.20 m (18 in. to 4 feet) — is the contact distance between close friends and family members. Conversations on important topics take place here. Personal distance can be illustrated by a family gathered around a dining table.

Social distance — 1.20 to 3.70 m (4 to 12 feet) — describes the distances at which conversations about work, vacation memories and other types of ordinary information can be exchanged. A living room suite around a coffee table is a good physical expression of this category of conversation.

Public distance — more than 3.70 m (12 feet) — describes the distance of more formal contact and one-way communication. This is the distance between teacher and pupil, pastor and congregation, and the distance we choose if we want to see or hear a street entertainer, but at the same

at arm's length

Like birds, people too want to keep a distance between individuals. One example of our preference for arm's length distance is shown by the way we line up at bus stops (Amman, Jordan; Chiba, Japan; and Montreal, Canada).

distance and communication

time want to signal that we do not want to be part of the happening. Wherever people communicate directly with others, we can see how they constantly use space and distance. We move closer, or lean forward, or withdraw discreetly. As well as physical distance, warmth and touching are other important parameters.

The significance of movement, distance and temperature are similarly reflected in language. We talk about coming over, going away, falling in love and backing out of situations. We speak of close friendships, near misses and distant relatives.

People can have warm feelings, heated discussions and hot dates. In contrast, we can send cold glances and icy stares and snub unwanted attention by giving it the cold shoulder.

We use these common ground rules for communication in all of life's situations. They help to initiate, develop, control and conclude relationships with people we know and don't know, and they help us signal when we do or do not want contact.

The existence of these communication ground rules is important in order for people to move securely and comfortably among strangers in public space.

at arm's length

Unlike many other species, man is a "do-not-touch" individual. Intimate distance is the zone for exchanging powerful emotional impressions, a zone where the presence of others is not wanted except by special invitation. The individual guards this zone, which can be described as an invisible, personal bubble. Everyone else is kept, quite literally, at arm's length.

The principle of arm's length distance — or at the very least don't touch distance — can be seen in all manner of contexts: at the beach, in parks, on benches, waiting for someone or something in town or in a queue waiting for the bus. Wherever physically possible the individual seeks to maintain the narrow but vital distance that keeps the situation secure and comfortable.

In crowds jostling to get on a bus or into an elevator, we handle the inevitable physical contact by stiffening our muscles and avoiding looking directly into other people's faces. While riding in the elevator we keep our arms flattened to our sides and our eyes most likely glued to the lighted panel showing which floor we're on. Initiating a conversation in an elevator is almost impossible, because there is no room to "back out" again.

Communication between people requires a reasonable amount of space. We have to be able to regulate, develop and wrap up events. If we're seated at a dining room table or around a coffee table, we can lean backward and forward and thus continually regulate the conversational distance by small increments. On streets and squares we can dance our

Below: a painted line is used to indicate a suitable public distance for tourists near the guardhouse (Royal Castle, Stockholm, Sweden).
Right: Respect for personal space is shown in choice of seats (Washington Square Park, New York City).

Narrow tables ensure a personal distance and encourage intense conversations. The very size of wider tables makes the occasion more formal.

way through an entire choreography by approaching, moving closer, weaving to and fro and at last backing gracefully out of the situation. A good conversation requires a certain amount of latitude. We're not talking about many meters (yards) here: just room to maneuver between social and personal distances.

For the same reason, stairways and landings do not provide a good conversational platform. There is seldom room to maneuver and there are often awkward differences in height to deal with, with one person standing a step or two above the other in order to establish a suitable distance. Conversations on an equal footing and with room to maneuver are always more comfortable.

communication and dimensions

A thorough knowledge of the senses and contact distances provides a valuable starting point for planning the dimensions and furnishing of a room. If a dinner party is held at narrow tables, a festive mood quickly catches on because everyone can talk in several directions across the tables. In other words, there are many partygoers within a comfortable personal distance. If the tables are very wide, people can only talk to the guests to their immediate right and left. If someone tries to open a conversation across a wide table, they have to raise their voice and other conversation stops. The unspoken assumption seems to be that the shouted message must be important since it is being conveyed in such a loud voice so publicly. Festivities are off to a slow start when the point of departure is a few people side by side and the others at a public distance. The whole event becomes more formal.

At community workshops it is common to see tables pushed hastily together into a block of four so people can work in groups. That way there is space for everyone in the group around the large table. However, the distance across the table is now so great that the group members can't really talk to each other. Everyone has to speak in a loud voice at the large tables, and in practice, group work done like this is poor. Small tables and many people sitting close together are a much better solution. Instead of public distance, we now have personal or social distance; voices can be toned down and nuances perceived.

Naturally, careful work with senses and distances is also important in a teaching situation. There has to be eye contact between teacher and pupil and as short a distance as feasibly possible to ensure intense, multifaceted communication.

"make sure there's never quite enough room"

"Make sure there's never quite enough room" was the universal advice regarding any teaching situation given by Sven-Ingvar Andersson, professor of landscaping at the School of Architecture, Royal Danish Academy of Art, from 1963 to 1994. "If you're expecting 100 students for a lecture, find a room that seats only 50." The room will fill up quickly, and everyone will think that this must be an important lecture indeed since so many people have turned up. The last students to arrive consider themselves lucky to have found even standing room. The atmosphere is concentrated and expectations are high. The distance between lecturer and students is as modest as possible during the lecture itself, making the experience more intense for everyone.

In the reverse situation, where 50 students are spread out in a hall that seats 300, everyone wonders why the other students haven't bothered to come. People start to speculate about whether something more important is happening elsewhere at the university. The atmosphere in the hall is slightly unfocused, and the lecture must be given over a far greater distance than necessary. No matter how well the lecture has been planned and is delivered, the whole séance will seem a bit tiring

A perfect room for a good talk about dailyday subjects. Wanting to provide a good social distance determined the size of the hot pots in the city's thermal baths (Reykjavik, Iceland).

Warm, intense contacts between people take place at short distances. Small spaces and short distances convey a corresponding experience of warm, intense city environments — regardless of weather (Kyoto, Japan; Perth, Australia; Farum, Denmark).

and uncommitted.

The connection between distance, intensity, closeness and warmth in various contact settings has an interesting parallel in decoding and experiencing cities and city space.

In narrow streets and small spaces, we can see buildings, details and the people around us at close range. There is much to assimilate, buildings and activities abound and we experience them with great intensity. We perceive the scene as warm, personal and welcoming.

This is in sharp contrast to the experience in cities and urban complexes where distances, urban space and buildings are huge, built-up areas are sprawled out, details are lacking and there are no or few people.

This type of urban situation is often perceived as impersonal, formal and cold. In places where built-up areas are large-scale and spread out, there generally isn't much to experience. And for the senses closely tied to strong, intense feeling, there is absolutely nothing.

Large spaces and large buildings signal an impersonal, formal and cool urban environment.

Scale confusion in Venice. While modern technology enables us to build large, it adds to confuse the understanding of the human scale (cruise ship seen from Via Garibaldi, Venice, Italy).

Scale shift at the Singapore River. The old four-to-five story buildings meet the new skyscrapers. It is easy to fantasize that the different buildings were envisioned for two different species. Not unexpectedly, almost all of the outdoor activities by the river take place in front of the low buildings.

The number of moving and parked cars has heavily contributed to the confusion in concepts concerning scale relations in cities.

too big, too tall and too fast

Traditional, organic cities grew on the basis of everyday activities over time. Travel was on foot, and construction was based on generations of experience. The result was cities on a scale adapted to the senses and potential of human beings.

Today urban planning decisions are made on the drawing board, and little time is lost between decision and realization. The speed of new forms of transport and the often massive scale of building projects pose new challenges. Traditional knowledge about scale and proportions has gradually been lost, with the result that new urban areas are often built on a scale far removed from what people perceive as meaningful and comfortable.

If we are to encourage pedestrian and cycle traffic and realize the dream of lively, safe, sustainable and healthy cities, we must begin with a thorough knowledge of the human scale. Understanding the scale of the human body is important if we are to work purposefully and appropriately with it as well as address the interplay between the small slow scale and the other scales also in operation.

cars and the shattered scale

The introduction of cars and car traffic has been decisive in creating confusion about scale and dimensions in cities. Cars fill a lot of space all on their own. Buses and trucks are almost all enormous, and even a small European compact car can seem dramatically large in a space created for the human body. Cars take up a lot of room when driving and a lot of room when parked. A parking lot for only 20 or 30 cars fills the same amount of space as a good little city square. And when speed in urban areas is increased from five to 60 or 100 km/h (three to 37 or 62 mph), all spatial dimensions increase dramatically, and images and visions for likely cityscapes follow along.

Cars and car traffic have been a pressing urban planning problem for more than 50 years. At the same time the sense of proportion and scale has gradually become more and more car oriented. The ability to work purposefully with the relationship between human scale and car scale as two distinct disciplines is seldom demonstrated, because the car problem has greatly confused the understanding of scale.

planning ideologies and the shattered scale

In parallel to the development of car traffic and building technology, planning ideologies have also followed suit by introducing huge distances,

Even a small car looms large in a medieval city and the school bus fills the entire street (Santiago Atitlán, Guatemala).

tall buildings and fast architecture. The modernist rejection of streets and the traditional city in the 1920s and 1930s and the introduction of functionalist ideals of hygienic, well-lit dwellings resulted in visions of the widespread tall city between freeways. Walking, cycling and meeting others in shared urban spaces were not part of these visions, which in subsequent decades had an immense impact on new urban development all over the world.

If at any time planners had been asked to design cities that would make life difficult and discourage people from being outdoors, it could hardly have been done more effectively than was the case for all the cities developed in the 20th century on this ideological basis

huge buildings, big thinking, large scale

Developments in society, economy and building technology have gradually resulted in urban areas and stand-alone buildings on an unprecedented scale. Greater wealth has spawned a greater need for space for all functions. Factories, offices, shops and housing: all units have grown. Building structures and commissions have grown correspondingly and the construction tempo is faster. Building technology has kept pace, with rational production methods that allow new broader, longer and higher edifices to be built. Whereas in the past cities were built by adding new buildings along public spaces, today new urban areas are often collections of random, spectacular stand-alone buildings between parking lots and large roads.

In the same period, architectural ideals have shifted their focus from elaborately detailed buildings erected in an urban context to spectacular individual works, often with a labored design idiom, built to be seen in a flash at great distance. The visions and thinking are large, just like the scale.

There are good financial, technological and ideological explanations for why modern cities look the way they do, and why planners and architects in general have become so confused and out of practice in working with the human scale.

In this context, it is interesting to note that throughout the period there were planners and architects who understood how to combine the new challenges with respect for human scale. Throughout his working life, Swedish-British architect Ralph Erskine (1914 – 2005) demonstrated ways of respecting the human scale in new buildings such as the Byker complex in Newcastle from 1969 – 1983.

The B001 complex in Malmø, Sweden (2001), the Aker Brygge quarter in Oslo, Norway (1986 – 1998) and housing in the new urban area Vauban in Freiburg, Germany (1986 – 2006) are other examples of new city districts designed with concern for the human scale.

Another category of buildings where consideration for the human scale is almost always in evidence is shopping centers, entertainment parks, restaurants and seaside hotels, where comfortable conditions for people are a prerequisite for financial success. These examples show that it is possible to work consciously with the human scale in various combinations with other scale requirements.

Architect Ralph Erskine's design of this complex reflects his mastery of both the large and small scale (Byker, Newcastle, England).

large buildings — small people

Lack of understanding and respecting the human scale impacts on the great majority of new cities and built-up areas. Buildings and city spaces grow increasingly larger but the people who are expected to use them are as always — small.
(La Defence, Paris; Eurolille, Lille, France; and Brasilia, Brazil).

When it is vital for customers and guests to feel welcome, every effort is made to keep the dimensions and design of outdoor space in harmony with the human scale (resort hotel by the Dead Sea in Jordan and "The Cappucino strip," Freemantle, Australia).

The challenge is that the principles of good human scale must be a natural part of the urban fabric in order to invite people to walk and cycle. For many reasons, in future we will have to build many large complexes and buildings with large dimensions and many stories. But neglecting the human scale is never an option.

The human body, senses and mobility are the key to good urban planning for people. All the answers are right here, encapsulated in our own bodies. The challenge is to build splendid cities at eye height with tall buildings rising above the beautiful lower stories.

"When in doubt, leave some meters (yards) out"

Faced with the very real temptation to design spaces too large for too few people, and the temptation to add a few extra meters (yards) to the spaces between buildings "for safety's sake," the advice in almost every case is to reduce size to conform to the adage: "When in doubt, leave some meters (yards) out."

3

The lively, safe, sustainable, and healthy city

Life in city space has a significant im-pact on how we perceive the space. A lifeless street is like an empty theater: something must be wrong with the production since there is no audience.

Life in the city is a relative concept. It is not the number of people that counts but the feeling that the place is popu-lated and being used (local streets in Brazil and the Netherlands and a city street in Flushing, New York).

3.1
The lively city

City life as process

the lively city
— and the lifeless

While the inviting, lively city can be a goal in itself, it is also the starting point for holistic city planning that encompasses the vital qualities that make a city safe, sustainable and healthy.

When planners aim for more than just ensuring that people can walk and bike in cities, focus expands from merely providing sufficient space for movement to the much more important challenge of enabling people to have direct contact with the society around them. In turn this means that public space must be alive, with many different groups of people using it.

Nothing makes a more poignant statement about the functional and emotional qualities of life and activity in the common space of the city than its opposite: the lifeless city.

The lively city sends friendly and welcoming signals with the promise of social interaction. The presence of other people in itself signals which places are worthwhile. A theater with a full house and a theater that is nearly empty send two completely different messages. One signals anticipation of a common, enjoyable experience. The other signals that something is amiss.

The lively city and the lifeless city also send completely different signals. Architectural perspective drawings, which always show groups of happy people between buildings regardless of the actual qualities of the projects depicted, also tell us that life in public places is a key urban attraction.

the lively city
— a relative concept

With the happy throngs of people in the architectural drawings in mind, it is important to clarify that the experience of liveliness in the city is not limited to quantity. The lively city is a relative concept. A few people in a narrow village street can easily present a lively, beckoning picture. It is not numbers, crowds and city size that matter but the sense that city space is inviting and popular that creates a meaningful place.

The lively city also needs varied and complex city life; where recreational and social activities are mixed with room for necessary pedestrian traffic as well as the opportunity to participate in urban life. Overfilled sidewalks with large crowds in transit jostling their way from place to place do not at all indicate good conditions for city life. While the discus-

life in the city — a self-reinforcing process

Nothing happens because nothing happens because nothing...
(Tuborg Harbor, Copenhagen).

Life in the city is a self-reinforcing process. Something happens because something happens because something happens. Once a children's game gets going, it can quickly attract more participants. Corresponding processes are at work with adult activities. People come where people are.

sion of the lively city revolves around quantity in the form of a meaningful minimum of participants, quality is an equally important concern and underscores the need for a multifaceted invitation.

life in the city —
a self-reinforcing process

Inviting cities must have carefully designed public space to support the processes that reinforce city life. One important prerequisite is that city life is a potentially self-reinforcing process.

"People come where people are" is a common saying in Scandinavia. People are spontaneously inspired and attracted by activity and the presence of other people. From the window, children see other children playing outside and hurry to join them.

one plus one quickly becomes
more than three

Combined with good habits and daily routines, good space and critical mass are prerequisites for processes in which small events can blossom. Once the process is underway, it is very much a positive spiral in which one plus one can quickly become more than three.

Something happens because something happens because...

We see quite the opposite in many areas with windy and ill-defined city space, with only a few people dispersed over a large area and few children "in the neighborhood." Under circumstances like these people are not in the habit of venturing out because the positive processes have never gained a foothold.

Nothing happens because nothing happens because...

concentrating or spreading
people and events

With people and events few and far between in many modern urban areas, there are fewer people and activities to populate city space. The potential of city life as a self-reinforcing process underscores the importance of careful urban planning that concentrates and breathes life into new urban areas.

Planning for events and parties has familiarized us with the principles of concentrating activities in order to kick start good processes. If we are expecting a limited number of guests, we need to concentrate them in a few rooms on the same floor. If things get a bit crowded, well, that is usually not a big problem — quite the contrary. If we try to spread this same event over many large rooms and perhaps even over several floors, it will almost inevitably fail to be memorable.

The principles that underlie successful events can be used in modern urban planning in places where we cannot count on a large number of visitors. Here we need to concentrate the people and activities in just a few rooms of suitable size and on the same level.

These simple principles have been used consistently in Venice, with its close-knit city structure and crowds of pedestrians. Although it has many streets, alleys and squares of all sizes, the basic structure is deceptively simple, concentrated around a limited number of main streets connecting key destinations and a strict hierarchy of major and minor

New residential areas are sparsely populated. A century ago seven times more people lived in the same amount of space.[1]

	1900 Old city areas	2000 New city ares (high density)	2000 New city ares (low density)	2000 New city areas (suburbs)
Average size of household	4 people	1.8 people	2 people	2.2 people
Average dwelling area per resident m²/sq. ft.	10/110	60/650	60/650	60/650
Floor to plot ratio	200%	200%	25%	20%
Number of dwellings per hectare	475	155	21	8
Number of residents per hectare	2,000 persons	280 persons	42 persons	17 persons

It is important to assemble people and events. However, too many and too large outdoor spaces are typically provided for new residential areas. The processes that encourage city life never have a chance to get started.

squares. The whole city is built around a simple network that provides the shortest routes and few but important spaces. When important spaces are few and routes logically follow the obvious desireable lines for walking, more effort can be put into the quality of the individual space.

Shops, restaurants, monuments and public functions can be logically placed where people are likely to be passing by. Walking distances seem shorter that way and the trip more of an experience. You get the opportunity to combine the useful with the pleasurable — and all by foot.

wanted: short logical routes, small spaces and a clear city space hierarchy

These are the exact qualities that can be used to advantage in modern urban planning. Key words for encouraging life in the city are: compact, direct and logical routes; modest space dimensions; and a clear hierarchy where decisions have been made about which spaces are the most important.

These principles contrast strongly with the urban planning practiced in many contemporary urban areas. Here planners typically build too much common space and make the individual spaces far too big. Streets, boulevards, alleys, avenues, paths, balconies, gardens, roof gardens, courtyards, squares, parks and recreational areas are generously strewn over plans with little thought given to natural sequences, which spaces are important, or the extent to which it is even meaningful to build them. In almost every case the result is too many square meters and spaces that are too large for too few visits. It is only on the architectural drawings that the same few people can be in so many different places at once. In fact everything has been done to prevent the positive spiral from ever really gaining a foothold.

Nothing happens because nothing happens because . . .

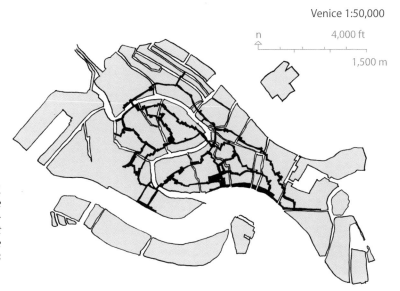

Venice 1:50,000

n

4,000 ft

1,500 m

Although it might look complicated, the network of main streets in Venice is both simple and compact. As directly as possible, the streets connect the city's most important hubs: the major bridges, the important squares and the transit terminals.

dense city, lively city
— a truth with qualifications

It is widely believed that the lively city needs high building density and large concentrations of dwellings and workplaces.

But what the lively city really needs is a combination of good inviting city space and a certain critical mass of people who want to use it. There are countless examples of places with high building density and poor city spaces that do not work at all. New urban areas are often dense and fully developed, but their city spaces are too numerous, too big and too impoverished to inspire anyone to venture into them.

In fact, we often see that poorly planned high density actually obstructs the establishment of good city space, thus quenching life in the city. Downtown Sydney is dominated by high-rise buildings. Many people live and work along dark, noisy streets with strong gusty winds. The streets allow people to get from one place to another, but are otherwise rather uninviting. New York City's Manhattan also has many examples of skyscraper clusters with dark, unattractive streets at their base.

reasonable density
and good quality city space

In contrast, Greenwich Village and Soho in New York City are less dense than Manhattan in general but still relatively high in density. The buildings are lower so the sun reaches into the tree-lined streets — and there is life. Building by building, having fewer floors and more attractive city space in these parts of New York City provides considerably more life than the high-density, high-rise areas where many more people live and work. Reasonable density and good quality city space are almost always preferable to areas with higher density, which often specifically inhibits the creation of attractive city space.

City life is a matter of quantity and quality. Density alone does not necessarily produce life in the streets. While many people live and work in high-density buildings, the surrounding city spaces may easily become dark and forbidding (Lower Manhattan, New York City).

Another problem that reduces city life around these high-rise buildings is that people on the top floors — of apartments as well as workplaces — venture into the city less often than those who live and work in the lower four to five floors. These lower floors give occupants visual contact with city space and the "trip" in and out is not perceived as so long and difficult.

Numerous studies of Danish housing areas show generally that developments with two- to two-and-a-half story town houses have considerable more street life and socializing per household than those with taller buildings.[2]

The conclusion is that erecting tall buildings to create very high density and poor public space is not a useful recipe for lively cities, even though contractors and politicians often use the argument of infusing life into the city for constructing tall dense building areas.

City life does not happen by itself or develop automatically simply in response to high density. The whole issue requires a targeted and considerably more varied approach. Lively cities require compact city structure, reasonable population density, acceptable walking and biking distances and good quality city space. Density, which represents quantity, must be combined with quality in the form of good city space.

There are many ways of applying an intelligent architectural approach to relatively high building density without making buildings too tall, streets too dark, and without constructing psychological barriers that discourage residents from making the "journey" from inside to outside.

Many older urban quarters demonstrate a combination of compact density and good city space, as exemplified by the city centers of Paris and Copenhagen. The world-famous Cerdà city structure in Barcelona also has fine city space, vibrant street life and actually a higher development density than Manhattan in New York City.

One outstanding new urban area is Aker Brygge on the waterfront in Oslo, Norway (1984 – 1992). Careful consideration was given to density, mix of functions and good city space. Despite a high building density (260%), the buildings do not seem tall, because those along the streets have fewer floors than those set further back.

City space is well proportioned with active ground floor frontages, and thanks in great part to the good design, the area has become one of the few new urban areas in Europe where people actually enjoy spending time. Density is high, but it is the right kind of density.

The Aker Brygge complex (1984 – 1992) in Oslo is one of the relatively few new built-up areas that has tall buildings, high-density, and good inviting city space. This combination has made the district very attractive and popular.

slow traffic means lively cities

Life in the city is very much a matter of numbers and time. There is life on the streets of pedestrian cities because people are present in the field of vision for a long time (Venice, Italy, and hutong in Beijing, China).

Fast-moving traffic on the motorway comprises many units but they are quickly out of sight. When traffic is moving slowly or grinds to a halt, there is much more to look at.

life in the city — a question of numbers and time

As already mentioned, it is widely believed that life in city space is largely a question of number of users, but the issue is not nearly that simple.

The number of users, the quantity, is one factor, but another equally significant factor for life in the city is the amount of time users spend in public city space. Life in city space as we experience it when moving about the city is a matter of how much there is to see and experience within the social visual field of about 100 meters (328 feet). The activity in the visual field is linked to how many other people are present and how much time each user spend at the site. The activity level is simply a product of number and time. Many people moving quickly through the space can result in considerably less life in the city than a handful of people who spend time there.

On Strøget, one of Copenhagen's main pedestrian streets, foot traffic is 35% slower in summer than in winter. This means that the same number of people provides a 35% increase in the activity level in the street.[3] It is generally true that the activity level in city space often increases dramatically in good weather. The difference is not that there are neccesarily more people in town, but that the individual user spends more time there. We walk slower, stop more often and are tempted by offers to stay a while on benches or in cafés.

slower traffic means lively cities

Recognizing that life in the city is a product of "how many" and "how long" helps us understand a number of urban phenomena. Calculating both number and time is a necessary planning tool for reinforcing life in cities.

Venice has a remarkably high level of activity although the population has been reduced dramatically. The explanation is that all traffic is on foot, everyone walks slowly and there are many spontaneous stays. The gondolas and other boat traffic also move at a pleasant tempo. So despite the small number of people and boats, there is always something to look at because slow traffic means lively cities.

In contrast, our many modern car-oriented suburbs contain far more people, but traffic moves quickly and few people stay. Cars move out of our field of vision almost before they enter it. This also explains why there is little to experience. Fast traffic results in lifeless cities.

One important argument in discussions about reorganizing traffic and traffic principles for streets is that there is more life in urban neighborhoods when people move slowly. The goal of creating cities where more people are invited to walk and bike will bring more life to the streets and a greater wealth of experience because fast traffic will be converted into slower traffic.

long outdoor stays mean lively cities

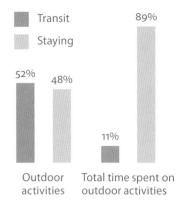

Transit

Staying

52%
48%
89%
11%

Outdoor activities

Total time spent on outdoor activities

A study of outdoor activities in 12 Canadian residential streets. "Come and go" activities make up more than half of the number of activities but are all very short in duration. Staying activities last an average of nine times longer and therefore contribute 89% of life in the streets.[4]

lengthy stays mean lively cities

Studies in Canada of a number of residential streets in Waterloo and Kitchener in 1977 recorded activities in public space. Half of all activities along the streets could be categorized as going to and from — whether by car, bicycle or on foot. The other half concerned people on or alongside the streets engaged in activities such as playing, maintenance, gardening, talking and sitting, the latter specifically residents in their front yards or porches following what was going on.

So as many people were going to and from as were staying near their homes. But going to and from did not take many seconds because the distance from the front door to the street corner was only 100 meters (328 feet). Nor did walking from car to front door on returning home take long — an average of 30 seconds, a fact that did not contribute much to life on the street.

In contrast, staying activities lasted considerably longer and various staying activities accounted for 89% of street life. Only 11% of life on the streets was due to purposeful movement. These statistics support the connection between lengthy outdoor stays and lively cities.[5]

A number of studies of city life conducted in new and old car-free squares in Copenhagen and Oslo underscore the importance of working with duration as well as numbers to create lively, attractive city space. The sites studied have on the order of 5,000 to 10,000 pedestrians daily. Nonetheless some of the sites seem deserted while others teem with life. The difference is simply that some squares only serve to ferry pedestrians from one side to the other, while others combine the opportunity to walk with staying, experiences and comfort. Squares that combine walking and staying register an activity level of between 10, 20 and sometimes even up to 30 times times higher than transit squares.[6] If lively and attractive cities are the goal, there is every reason to look at staying opportunities and attractions.

more people
— or more minutes?

At a time when politicians, contractors, realtors and architectural draftsmen are showing a commendable interest in ensuring lively and attractive cities, it must be pointed out that focus on high-rises and compact density barely skirts the issues — and not even the most crucial ones at that.

In a given situation life in the city can be influenced quantitatively by inviting more people to come or qualitatively by inviting them to stay longer and slowing down traffic. It is almost always simpler and more effective to increase quality and thus the desire to spend time than to increase the number of visitors to the space.

Working with time and quality rather than numbers and quantity also generally improves city quality for the benefit of everyone every day of the year.

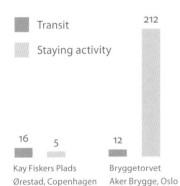

Transit

Staying activity

212

16   5   12

Kay Fiskers Plads   Bryggetorvet
Ørestad, Copenhagen   Aker Brygge, Oslo

The bar graph shows the average number of people who stay on two newly built squares in Copenhagen and Oslo respectively, on summer days between 12 noon and 4 pm.
Top right: Pedestrians race through this square between the Metro station and a shopping center in under a minute (Kay Fiskers Plads, Ørestad, Copenhagen, Denmark).
Below right: The activity level at this square on a typical summer day is 10 times greater because the public is invited both to walk and to stay here. (Bryggetorget, Oslo, Norway).[7]

the edge — where building and city meet

Chatting by

Entering and leaving

Walking alongside

Standing alongside

Taking a break by

Standing in doorways

Shopping next to

Interacting with

Looking at displays with

Sitting on

Sitting next to

Looking in and out of

where city and building meet

The treatment of the city's edges, particularly the lower floors of buildings, has a decisive influence on life in city space. This is the zone you walk along when you're in town, and these are the frontages you see and experience close up and therefore intensely. This is where you enter and leave buildings, where indoor and outdoor life can interact. This is where city meets building.

edges that define space

The edges of a city limit the visual field and define individual space. Edges make a vital contribution to spatial experience and to the awareness of individual space as a place. Just as the walls of a home support activities and communicate a sense of well being, the city's edges offer a feeling of organization, comfort and security. We recognize space with no edges or weak edges from many urban squares with heavily trafficked roads on all four sides. Their function is considerably more impoverished than the city space where life is directly reinforced by one or more attractive edges.[8]

edges as exchange zone

The edge along ground floors is also a zone in which doors and exchange points between inside and outside are located. The edges provide the opportunity for life in the buildings or immediately in front of the buildings to interact with life in the city. This is the zone where activities inside the buildings can move out into the common space of the city.

edges as staying zone

The edge zone also offers some of the city's prime opportunities for sitting and standing. The local climate is best here, our backs are protected, and our frontal sensory apparatus can comfortably master the situation. We have a full view of everything going on in the space and are in no danger of unpleasant surprises from behind. The edge is a really good place to be in a city.

The general tendency for people to keep to walls is confirmed in public as well as private space, both indoors and out. You could say that life grows from the edge in towards the middle. At dances we talk about wallflowers lining the walls between dances. At receptions guests typically hug the walls and only later move more freely around the room. Children begin their outdoor activities by hanging around the front door, only taking over the entire space when play starts. In pauses between activities, children once use again the edge zone for waiting and watching until a new game or activity gets underway.

People who have to wait in public spaces find good spots along the edges for lingering. Edge placements are also carefully selected for longer stays on benches or at sidewalk cafés. Our backs are protected when

In the French colonial period, regulations ensured narrow units and many doors throughout the city of Hanoi, Vietnam. This principle can also be recommended for new built-up areas (Sluseholmen, Copenhagen, Denmark (2007 – 2009)).

All over the world the same rhythms are found in attractive shopping streets: 15 to 20 shops per 100 meter/328 feet of street means new experiences for pedestrians every four to five seconds (Changcha, China; Middlesbrugh, UK; and New York City).

we sit along the edge and good view of the space is in offer. When the edge also has umbrellas and awnings, we can have an overview yet still be hidden in the shade. Obviously, this is a good place to be.

city edges as experience zone

As pedestrians, we experience ground floors closely and intensely. The upper floors are not part of our immediate field of vision, nor are the buildings on the other side of the street. We view the floors above us and the buildings across the street from a considerably greater distance, and for the same reason our perception of them lacks detail and intensity.

The situation is quite different for the ground floors we pass while walking. We intensely appreciate all the details of the façades and display windows. We experience close-up the rhythms of the façade, the materials, colors and people in or near the buildings and they largely determine whether our walk is interesting and eventful. For city planners there are heavy arguments in favor of concentrating on ensuring active and interesting ground floors along important walking routes. In terms of visual and other types of experience, all the other elements play a far less significant role.

good rhythms — fine details

Walking in the city leaves ample time to experience everything that ground floors have to offer and to savor the wealth of detail and information. Walks become more interesting and meaningful, time passes quickly and distances seem shorter.

However, where there are no interesting edges to skirt or where ground floors are closed and monotonous, walks seem long and impoverished in terms of experience. The whole process can become so meaningless and tiring that people give up walking altogether.

Physiological studies of people in a room with no stimulation show that our senses need stimulation at fairly short intervals of four to five seconds, which appears to ensure a reasonable balance between too few and too many stimuli.[9] It is interesting to note that shops and booths in active, thriving commercial streets all over the world often have a façade length of five or six meters (16 – 20 feet), which corresponds to 15 – 20 shops or other eye-catching options per 100 meters (328 feet). At an ordinary walking speed of about 80 seconds per 100 meters (328 feet), the façade rhythm on these streets means that there are new activities and sights to see about every five seconds.

narrow units — many doors, please

The principle of many narrow units and many doors along commercial streets provides the best opportunities for buyers and sellers to interact, and the numerous doors provide many exchange points between inside and out. There is much to experience and room for many tempting offers. Not surprisingly, many new shopping malls also use the principle. of narrow units with many doors. This too makes room for many shops along walkways.

and with vertical relief in the façades, please

But where shops are located on the ground floor and at the many other edges in cities where housing or other functions are accommodated, it is important to ensure that the ground-floor façades have vertical façade articulation. This ploy makes walking distances seem shorter and more interesting. In contrast, façades designed with long horizontal lines make distances seem longer and more tiring.

soft edges — and hard

Scale and Rhythm
The 5 km/h – 3 mph scale, compact and full of interest with narrow units and many doors.
The 60 km/h – 37 mph scale works for drivers on the move, but not for pedestrians.

5 km/h – 3 mph

or 60 km/h – 37 mph scale

Transparency
Walking in the city is enhanced for pedestrians if they can see goods on display and what is going on inside buildings. And that works both ways.

Open

or closed

Appeal to Many Senses
All our senses are activated when we are close to buildings that provide interesting impressions and opportunities.
In contrast, eight posters do not inspire.

Interactive

or passive

Texture and Details
City buildings hold attractions for pedestrians walking slowly. Appealing ground floors offer texture, good materials and a wealth of details.

Interesting

or boring

Mixed Functions
Narrow units and many doors supplemented by a wide variation in functions provide many points of exchange between in and out and many types of experiences.

Varied

or uniform

Vertical Façade Rhythms
Ground floors with primarily vertical façade rhythms make walks more interesting. They seem shorter too, compared to walks along horizontally oriented façades.

Source: "Close encounters with buildings," Urban Design International, 2006.

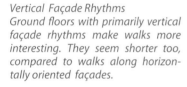

Vertical

or horizontal

soft edges – and hard

Narrow units, many doors and vertical relief in the façades help intensify the walking experience. Ground-floor activities and functional interaction with life on the street also have significant impact on city life.

To keep things simple, we can describe opportunities for experience from two extremes. One extreme is the street with a "soft edge" with shops lined up, transparent façades, large windows, many openings and goods on display. Here there is much to see and touch, providing many good reasons to slow down or even stop. The other extreme, the street with a "hard edge," is a diametrical contrast: the ground floors are closed and the pedestrian walks past long sections of façades of black glass, concrete or masonry. There are few or no doors and all in all little to experience or even reason to choose that particular street, short of necessity.

seven times more city life in front of active façades

Over the years many studies have been conducted on the impact of edge quality on city life, and they point to a direct connection between soft edges and lively cities. A study conducted in Copenhagen in 2003 looked at the extent of activities in front of an active and a passive façade section in several city streets.[10]

In front of the open and active façades there was a noticeable tendency for pedestrians to slow down and turn their heads towards the façade, and they stopped frequently. In front of the closed façade sections the walking tempo was markedly higher, and there were fewer turned heads and stops. In conclusion it could be shown that with the same stream of pedestrians in the active and passive street segments, the average number of people who walked by or stopped in front of active façade sections was seven times greater than the activity level in front of the passive façades. This is because people walked more slowly, made more stops and walked more often to and from the shops on the street with the soft edge.

A 2003 study of Copenhagen shopping streets shows that the activity level in front of active façade is seven times greater than in front of passive façades.[11]

an active ground-floor policy, please

According to the sign, the supermarket is open seven days a week, but certainly not towards the sidewalk (Adelaide, Australia).

Before and after photos of a street corner in Melbourne and a street in Stockholm. Both cities have adopted active façade policies.

It is perhaps even more interesting that numerous other activities unrelated to shops and façades also took place on this active street segment. People talked more on their cell phones, stopped to tie their shoes, organized their shopping bags and conversed to a far greater extent than in front of the passive façades. Very much in keeping with the principle that city life processes are often self-reinforcing: "People come where people are."

closed ground-floor façades
— lifeless cities

City streets with soft edges have a significant influence on activity patterns and the attractiveness of city space. The transparent, welcoming and active façades give city space a fine human scale just where it means most: up close and at eye level.

The quality of ground floors is so crucial to a city's overall appeal that it is difficult to understand why ground floors in many new and old cities are treated with such diffidence. Long closed walls, few doors, sterile glass sections that signal "move on" have propagated in cities, giving pedestrians numerous good reasons to give up and go home.

lively cities need an active
ground-floor policy

As part of efforts to improve the quality of the city environment in central Stockholm, a scale for mapping the attractiveness of the ground floors was drawn up in 1990.[12] The assessment method was later refined in the course of corresponding projects in other cities.

Mapping the attractiveness of ground floors can pinpoint problem areas in the city and be used to assess the situation in the city's most important streets. With this information as a platform, city planners can draw up an active, targeted ground-floor policy to ensure the attractiveness of the ground floors in new developments and address and gradually correct problems in the existing building mass, particularly along the most important pedestrian routes in the city.

In Melbourne just such a ground-floor policy has led to significant improvements, and a number of other cities and areas are making targeted

Registration of problem ground-floor façades in Copenhagen and Stockholm. In the 1950s and 1960s, inner Stockholm was subjected to extensive urban renovation. Buildings from that period often have dismissive façades, a problem that this registration clearly pinpoints (the registration method is shown on page 241).[13]

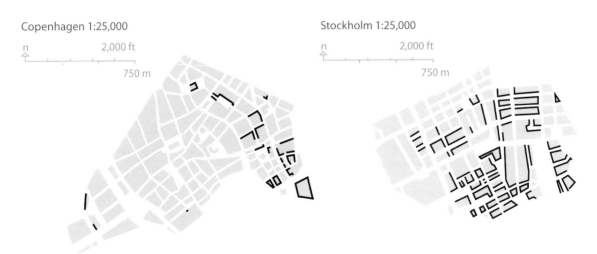

Copenhagen 1:25,000

n
2,000 ft

750 m

Stockholm 1:25,000

n
2,000 ft

750 m

efforts to deal with the issue. Plans for the new urban areas along Oslo's waterfront highlight the stretches and places where attractive ground floors will be crucial to future city quality. One way to make sure that plans are carried out is to reduce the rent in those ground floor areas that are critical to the attractiveness of the quarter. If the quarter is popular and attractive, overall rental income will be easily generated by the other properties.

soft edges
— in residential areas

The edge — where building and city meet — is also vital to the quality of housing and the vitality of the surrounding urban area. The edge zone is the most active outdoor area in a residential area. Here are front doors — the exchange zone between the private and public spheres — and this is where the activities from the residential areas move out to the terrace or front garden, in good contact with public space. The edge zone is also the one pedestrians see and experience when they walk through the area.

The significance of the edge zone can be summed up in the good advice given to the author by architect Ralph Erskine (1914 – 2005): "If the complex is interesting and exciting at eye level, the whole area will be interesting. Therefore try to make the edge zone inviting and rich in good detail, and save your efforts on the upper floors, which have far less importance both functionally and visually."[14]

Many places around the world offer interesting examples of the design and use of edge zones in residential areas: the front gardens of English semidetached houses, Dutch "stoops," edge zones by traditional Japanese city houses, the North American "porch," steps and landings leading up to Brooklyn's brownstones in New York City, and the front yards of the low-rise row houses in Australian cities. All are examples of designs of semiprivate zones in older residential neighbourhoods. Quite a few new complexes worldwide also have inspiring examples of carefully designed edge zones in residential areas.

However, many new residential areas have allowed parking places and garages to usurp edge zones. Or they have done away with all ground-floor articulation, so that houses rise up from lawns and sidewalks like cliffs from the sea. People who live in this type of housing move directly from the private to the public sphere with no transition or variation.

soft edges
— and life on residential streets

Numerous studies proclaim the importance of semiprivate front yards and staying zones for life and activity on residential streets. In 1976 the University of Melbourne conducted an extensive study of 17 residential streets, some in older quarters with semidetached houses, some in suburbs with single-family dwellings. The study was based on detailed observations over entire days and included areas with and without semiprivate front yards. The study provided a comprehensive look at the nature of the activities on the streets, as well as the exact location of the

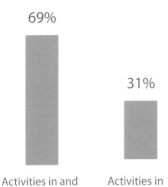

69%

31%

Activities in and
at front yards

Activities in
street space

The impact of soft edges is unmistakeable in the study of outdoor activities on 17 residential streets in Melbourne, Australia. Of all the registered activities, 69% took place in or around the semiprivate front yards. The remaining 31% of the activities took place in the streets.[15]

activities.

The streets with the most extensive activity level were the older residential streets with densely built townhouses and small, meticulously designed outdoor terraces between the dwelling and the sidewalk. Of all the activities — coming and going, staying, maintenance, conversations and play — 69% took place in the front yards or near the hedge and gates to the front yard. Only 31% of the activities took place in the other parts of the street space. A substantial portion of the activities combined staying outside — resting, drinking coffee and enjoying sunshine — with the opportunity to follow life on the street.[16]

The prerequisite for street life was the building density, which encouraged many people to get around the area by foot. Only when there is a certain amount of life on foot in front of the houses does it become meaningful and interesting to spend time on the public side of the houses. In areas with front yards and outdoor terraces in front of the housing units, but primarily car traffic on the roads, almost no one stayed outside in front of the residences.

Researchers carried out a series of studies in Waterloo and Kitchener, Canada, in 1977 with focus on typical North American residential streets with rather densely built family dwellings with a porch and yard fronting the street. They found an activity pattern that answered very closely to the pattern of the Australian residential streets. When the time spent on the various activities was studied, it turned out that it was activities carried on in or near the semiprivate edge zones that accounted for almost

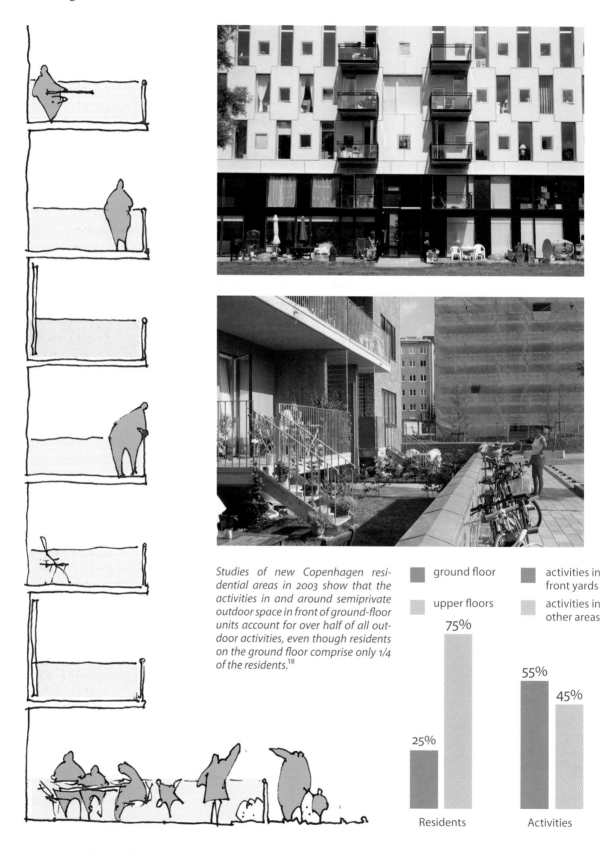

Studies of new Copenhagen residential areas in 2003 show that the activities in and around semiprivate outdoor space in front of ground-floor units account for over half of all outdoor activities, even though residents on the ground floor comprise only 1/4 of the residents.[18]

- ground floor
- upper floors
- activities in front yards
- activities in other areas

Residents: 25% / 75%

Activities: 55% / 45%

89% of life on the streets.[17] As mentioned earlier, it is the number of minutes spent outside per day rather than the number of people outside that determines whether a street is lively or lifeless. In the semiprivate front yards some of the private sphere activities can be introduced into the edge zone. It is safe, comfortable and people have visual contact with their surroundings, which naturally is important to life on the street in general.

A series of studies conducted in residential streets in Copenhagen in 1982 illustrates the situation in streets of row houses with and without front yards. The studies were conducted on parallel streets with identical dwellings and comparable categories of residents. In all of the studies the activity level in the streets with soft edges was between two and three times higher than in corresponding streets with hard edges.[19]

soft edges
— in new residential areas

A study of activity patterns in new residential areas conducted in Copenhagen in 2005 shows how balconies, front yards and other types of outdoor area are used in a contemporary urban context. The studies illustrate a general tendency for outdoor activities to shift from public to more private space. As in earlier studies, this study shows that the semiprivate outdoor space immediately in front of ground-floor level residences continues to play a remarkable role for the overall level of life in residential areas.

In the areas studied, street-level residences with a semiprivate front area comprised between 25% and 33% of the total number of residences, while the activities in these semiprivate front yards comprised 55% of all registered activities in the areas.[20] It is interesting that the front yards, where proximity to residence, space, plants and good local climate can be combined with contact with surroundings, were used far more than balconies where space, climate and contact are poorer.

Soft edges in front of residences have a crucial impact on the extent of outdoor activities (hard edges in a Norwegian housing area and soft edges in Solbjerg Have, Frederiksberg in Denmark).

Soft edges in older urban areas (Tokyo, Japan; Sydney, Australia; and Montreal, Canada).

Right: Soft edges throughout the district (The French Quarter in New Orleans, Louisiana).

Soft edges in new urban areas (Bogota, Colombia and Cape Town, South Africa).

Opposite page: street life near houses and front yards (Jakarta, Indonesia).

soft edges
— in various cultural contexts

In studies conducted over three decades on several continents in large and small cities, city centers and suburbs are mentioned above. Naturally the studies include areas and households representing a wide spectrum of cultures, living conditions and economic standards. In addition, usage patterns and housing cultures change over time in step with changes in lifestyle, buying power and demography. A well-rounded discussion about the function of soft edges in a residential context must then include cultural and socioeconomic dimensions. However, we will not take up this discussion here, where the subject is a more general illustration of the importance of soft edges for patterns of activity in city and housing areas, of options for people walking trough these areas and of the possibilities for contact between indoor and outdoor activities.

One m² (11 sq. feet) adjacent to home or ten m² (108 sq. feet) around the corner?

The studies mentioned above show an unambiguous picture of the soft edges as a simple and valuable element of city architecture that makes a inviting contribution in every area mentioned. The easier and more inviting it is to use city space or the edge of city space, the more lively it will be. In almost all situations, one m² (11 sq. feet) adjacent to home is more useful and used more often than 10 m² (108 sq. feet) around the corner.

lively cities with soft edges, please

No single topic has greater impact on the life and attractiveness of city space than active, open and lively edges. When the rhythms of the city's buildings produce short units, many doors and carefully designed details at ground-floor level, they support life in the city and near buildings. When the city's edges work, they reinforce city life. Activities can supplement each other, the wealth of experience increases, walking becomes safer and distances seem shorter.

In his book *A Pattern Language* (1977), Christopher Alexander summarizes the importance of edges by saying: "If the edge fails, then the space never becomes lively."[21]

It can — almost — be said that simply.

If only the edges work… Shopping street in Camden, London, and a residential area with steps (Brooklyn, New York).

lively cities — and lifeless

The previous chapter on senses and scale, describes how planning principles featuring large-scale traffic solutions and introverted buildings in combination with widespread scale confusion have resulted in impersonal and dismissive cities. These deserted and discouraging cities are a biproduct of planning that has had other priorities.

City life was a matter of course in old traditional cities until the mid-1950s. In fact, city life was taken for granted, and for good reason. Now in many parts of the world, city life is no longer a matter of course, but a valuable and relatively limited resource that city planners must manage carefully. Changes in society and planning methods have since drastically changed the situation.

In this chapter, attempts have been made to outline the methods that can be used to strengthen life in cities. Various tools are offered as ways of bolstering the human dimension depending on the situation and job at hand.

lively cities
— the product of careful planning

City vitality and tranquility are both desirable and valuable urban qualities. Peace and quiet are highly valued qualities in the lively active city . Arguments promoting the lively city should not aim specifically on creating as much life in the city as possible in as many places as possible.

The problem, however, is that desolate areas arise unaided in new urban areas. No one has to try very hard to achieve this result. It takes careful and concentrated effort to ensure a combination of lively and quiet places in the city.

When the goal is to develop cities, when the human dimension and the meeting between people are prioritized, when you wish to invite people to walk and bike, it is essential to work carefully to encourage life in cities.

It is important to remember that the answer is not to be found in simple, fixed principles about greater development density and getting more people in buildings, but in working carefully on many fronts with city life as a process and the main attraction.

Processes, invitations, city quality, the all-important time factor and inviting soft edges are key words for this work.

the price of fear

Since cars conquered the streets, fear and worry have become an integral part of daily life in cities the world over.

Bicyclists are in an extremely vulnerable position in many cities that still lack a good bicycle infrastructure. This sign from Japan shows that bicycling on sidewalks is not a good alternative.

3.2
The safe city

The safe city

The safe city

feeling safe in the city
— a vital city quality

Feeling safe is crucial if we hope to have people embrace city space. In general, life and people themselves make the city more inviting and safe in terms of both experienced and perceived security.

In this section we deal with the safe city issue with the goal of ensuring good cities by inviting walking, biking and staying. Our discussion will focus on two important sectors where targeted efforts can satisfy the requirement for safety in city space: traffic safety and crime prevention.

Safety and traffic

more room for cars
— as a dominant city policy?

In the more than 50 years since cars seriously invaded cities, both car traffic and the accident rate have increased apace. Fear of traffic accidents has risen even more sharply, with a dramatic impact on pedestrians and bicyclists and their enjoyment as they move about the city. As more cars have filled the streets, politicians and traffic planners have become increasingly focused on making room for even more car traffic and parking.

Conditions for pedestrians and cyclists have deteriorated as a result. Narrow sidewalks have gradually become filled with traffic signs, parking meters, bollards, street lamps and other obstacles placed there so as "not to be in the way." Understood as "in the way of the more important motorized traffic." Added to physical obstacles are the frequent interruptions in walking rhythm caused by long waits at stoplights, difficulty crossing streets, bleak underground tunnels and elevated pedestrian bridges. All of these examples of city organization have one purpose: to provide more room and better conditions for cars. As a consequence, walking has become more difficult and far less attractive.

Conditions for bicycles are even worse in many places: bike paths have been eliminated altogether or dangerous so-called "bike routes" painted on the road next to fast-moving cars, or there is a total absence of infrastructure for bicyclists, who must manage as best they can.

pedestrian-priority streets, please

The concept of shared or complete streets suggests equality between traffic groups, which is a utopian ideal. Integrating various types of traffic is not satisfactory until pedestrians are given a clear priority (shared space in Haren, the Netherlands, and a pedestrian priority street in Copenhagen, Denmark).

Throughout this entire period of car encroachment, cities have tried to remove bicycle traffic from their streets. The risk of accident to pedestrians and bicyclists has been great throughout the rise in car traffic, and the fear of accident even greater.

major differences in various parts of the world — but exactly the same problems

Many European countries and North America experienced the car invasion early on and have watched city quality deteriorate year by year. There have been numerous counter reactions and an incipient development of new traffic planning principles in response. In other countries whose economies have developed more slowly and modestly, cars have only begun to invade cities more recently. In every case the result is a dramatic worsening of conditions for pedestrians and bicycle traffic.

In cities where the car invasion began early and has lasted decades, we can now see a strong reaction against the myopic focus on cars that has dealt such harsh blows to city life and bicycle traffic.

modern traffic planning ensures better balance between types of traffic

In many countries, especially in Europe, traffic planning in the 21st century has changed dramatically compared to the traffic planning of twenty or thirty years ago. The importance of promoting pedestrian and bicycle traffic has gradually been acknowledged while better understanding of the nature and causes of traffic accidents has produced a considerably wider variety of planning tools.

When the first pedestrian streets were introduced in Europe in the 1960s, there were really only two street models: those for vehicular traffic and those for pedestrians. Numerous types of streets and traffic solutions have since been developed so that today's traffic planners have quite a wide range of streets to choose from: vehicular traffic-only streets, boulevards, 30 km/h (19 mph) traffic, pedestrian priority, 15 km/h (9 mph) areas, pedestrian-streetcar, pedestrian-bicycle and pedestrian only. The experience gained in the intervening years has also made it possible to reduce the number of traffic accidents and make walking or biking considerably safer and more comfortable.

In choosing street types and traffic solutions, it is important to start with the human dimension. People must be able to move comfortably and safely in cities on foot or by bicycle, and when traffic solutions are adopted special consideration must be given to children, the young, the elderly and people with disabilities. Quality for people and pedestrian safety must be key concerns.

pedestrians must have priority in mixed traffic

A number of recent urban planning ideologies deriving from accident statistics contend that the risk of accident can be reduced by physically mixing types of traffic in the same street under the heading of "shared space."

The underlying idea of these so-called shared streets is that they will give trucks, cars, motorcycles, bicycles and pedestrians of all ages the opportunity to travel quietly, side by side and with good eye contact. Serious accidents will rarely occur under such conditions, or so it is thought, because pedestrians and bicyclists need to be extra vigilant at all times.

Obviously, if people are sufficiently frightened and keep a close watch on traffic, nothing untoward will happen. However, the price is high in terms of dignity and quality. Children cannot be allowed free rein, and older people and others with reduced mobility may be forced to drop walking altogether. In any discussion about people and traffic safety the risk of accident must be weighed against quality for pedestrians and bicyclists. Much of modern traffic planning continues to pay far too little attention to the quality of city life.

Mixing types of traffic is certainly possible, but not on the equal terms implied by the shared street concept. As the British "home zones," Dutch "woonerfs," and Scandinavian "sivegader" have demonstrated for years, pedestrians can thrive with other forms of traffic as long as it is crystal

Copenhagen-style bicycle lanes take advantage of parked cars to protect bicyclists (street scenes from Copenhagen, Denmark).

The principle of having bicyclists bike outside a lane of parked cars does not solve many safety and security problems. It does help to protect the parked cars, however!

clear that all movement is based on the premises of pedestrians. Mixed–traffic solutions must prioritize either pedestrians or provide appropriate traffic segregation.[22]

pragmatic, flexible and considerate traffic planning

There is every reason to applaud the many new types of streets and policies that ensure safety for pedestrians and bicyclists while allowing service vehicles to make door-to-door deliveries.

From project to project, planners must consider which types of streets and degree of traffic integration would be a good solution. The actual and perceived safety of pedestrians must always be the determining factor. It is not a natural law that motorized traffic should be allowed access everywhere. It is generally accepted that cars are not welcome in parks, libraries, community centers and houses. The advantages to not having car traffic everywhere are obvious, so even though there are compelling arguments for allowing car traffic all the way to the front door, in many situations there are equally good arguments for establishing car-free areas surrounding the residences.

the Venice principle
— as inspiration

For centuries traffic in Venice has functioned on the principle that the transition from rapid to slow traffic does not take place at the front door but at the city limit. The Venice principle is hard to beat when prioritizing city quality. As mentioned above, a number of options have been developed for coexistence between pedestrian and motorized traffic. While these options open new doors, they also create more problems.

A pedestrian in Venice can be forgiven for thinking that many of the recent traffic solutions represent various forms of compromise compared to the vision of a true city for people. Or put in another way, in Venice it is easy to surmise that "there is only one thing better than slow cars — and that is no cars."

In Venice the shift from rapid to slow traffic occurs at the city limits rather than at the front door. This is an interesting and inspiring for the contemporary vision of creating lively, safe, sustainable and healthy cities.

But as also mentioned, it is important to be pragmatic and flexible. There are many good new compromises, but they must be assessed and carefully selected.

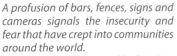

A profusion of bars, fences, signs and cameras signals the insecurity and fear that have crept into communities around the world.
Above right: Apartment block in Beijing, China.

Right: residential streets in Lima, Peru, converted to gated communities.

Safety and security

safe city — open city

Already in the first chapter of her 1961 book *The Death and Life of Great American Cities*, Jane Jacobs discusses the importance of safety in the streets. She describes the crime-preventive effect of life in the street, of mixing functions in buildings and of residents' care for common space.[23] Her expressions "street watchers" and "eyes on the street" have since become integral to city planning terminology.

Being able to walk safely in city space is a prerequisite for creating inviting well-functioning cities for people. Experienced as well as perceived safety is crucial for life in the city.

The safety discussion has a general and a more detailed dimension. The general focus is maintaining and supporting the vision of an open society in which people from all socioeconomic groups can move about side by side in the common room of the city as they go about their daily business. Within this general framework, safety can also be promoted through careful consideration for the design of the many detailed solutions in the city.

safety and society

Juxtaposed with the idealistic visions of safe open cities is the reality of many urban societies. Social and economic inequality is the backdrop for high crime rates and the fully or semiprivate attempts to protect property and private life.

Barbed wire and iron bars fortify houses, security patrols cruise residential areas, security guards stand in front of shops and banks, signs threaten "armed response" outside houses in exclusive quarters, gated communities abound: all of these are examples of people's attempts to protect themselves against invasion and trespass of private property. The examples also illustrate a general retreat to the private sphere by some population groups.

It is important to point out that simple individual urban crime-prevention solutions are not of much help, where the invasive sense of insecurity is often deeply rooted in social conditions. On the other hand, many urban communities are less gridlocked, including hard-hit city districts. In these areas there is every reason to make a solid effort to avoid the retreat of the population behind bars and barbed wire.

Other parts of the world do have cities and societies in which cultural tradition, family networks and social structure keep crime low despite economic inequalities.

To conclude, in almost all situations there are good arguments for working carefully to reinforce real and perceived safety, a prerequisite for using common city space.

The light from buildings along city streets can make a significant contribution to the feeling of security when darkness falls. Above: Bakery in Amman, Jordan, and Apple Store in Sydney, Australia.

Seven thousand people live in central Copenhagen, and on an ordinary weekday evening during the winter there are approximately seven thousand lighted windows visible from the street.[24]

If we shift the focus from defending the private sphere to a general discussion about feeling safe while walking in public space, we will find a clear-cut connection between the goal to strengthen city life and the desire for safety.

life in the city means safer cities — and safe cities provide more life

If we reinforce city life so that more people walk and spend time in common spaces, in almost every situation both real and perceived safety will increase. The presence of others indicates that a place is acceptly good and safe. There are "eyes in the street" and often "eyes on the street" as well because it has become meaningful and interesting for people in nearby buildings to follow what is going on in the street. When people make their daily rounds in city space, both the space and the people who use them becomes more meaningful and thus more important to keep an eye on and watch out for. A lively city becomes a valued city and thus also a safer city.

life in buildings means safer streets

Life in the street has an impact on safety, but life along the street also plays a significant role. Urban areas with mixed functions provide more activities in and near buildings around the clock. Housing in particular signifies good connections to the city's important common space and a marked reinforcement of the real and perceived safety in the evening and at night. So even if the street is deserted, lights from windows in residential areas send a comforting signal that people are nearby.

Approximately 7,000 residents live in Copenhagen's city center. On an ordinary weekday evening in the winter season a person walking through the city can enjoy the lights from about 7,000 windows.[25] The proximity to housing and residents plays a key role in the feeling of safety. It is common practice for city planners to mix functions and housing as a crime prevention strategy and thus increase the feeling of safety along the most important streets used by pedestrians and bicyclists. The strategy works well in Copenhagen, where the city center has buildings between five and six stories high, and there is good visual contact between residences and street space. The strategy does not work as well in Sydney. Although the Australian metropolis has 15,000 people living in its heart, the residences are generally from 10 to 50 stories above street level, no one who lives high up can see what is happening down on the street.

soft edges mean safer cities

Ground floor building design has a disproportionately large impact on the life and appeal of city space. Ground floors are what we see when we walk past buildings. It is also from the lower floors that people inside can follow what is going on outside, and vice versa.

If ground floors are friendly, soft and — in particular — populated, pedestrians are surrounded by human activity. Even at night when little is happening in cafés and front yards, furniture, flowers, parked bicycles and forgotten toys are a comforting witness of life and proximity to other people. Light streaming from the windows of shops, offices and dwellings at night helps increase the feeling of safety in the street.

Soft edges signal to people that a city is welcoming. In contrast, in streets with retail, where solid metal shutters close off shops outside opening hours a sense of rejection and insecurity is produced. The streets are dark and deserted in the evening, and there is not much reason to be there on weekends and holidays either. Given the general desire for safe cities and inviting ground floors, preferred façade options

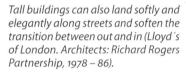

Tall buildings can also land softly and elegantly along streets and soften the transition between out and in (Lloyd´s of London. Architects: Richard Rogers Partnership, 1978 – 86).

Soft edges in a Chinese shopping street and a residential area in Frederiksberg, Denmark. In any case, soft transitions mean more activities in outdoor space and greater security.

have open metal grills and other types of transparency to protect goods but allow light to stream onto the street, and the also give nocturnal pedestrians the pleasure of window shopping.

ordinary concern means safer cities

Life in the street and on the street, mixed functions along the street and friendly edge zones are key qualities for good cities — also in terms of safety and protection. The polar opposite is the perfect recipe for an insecure urban environment: lifeless streets, mono-functional buildings devoid of activity for most of the day, closed, lifeless and dark façades. To this list we can add insufficient lighting, deserted paths and pedestrian tunnels, dark nooks and crannies, and too many bushes.

In the face of this rather depressing scenario it is important to remember that almost any enticement to invite people to walk, bicycle and stay in city space will also contributes to a greater sense of security.

clear structures mean safer cities

Another contribution to our sense of security is a good city layout that makes it is easy for us to find our way around. It is a mark of good urban quality when we can directly find the destination we're looking for without hesitation and detours. Clear structure and organization do not require large dimensions and broad straight roads from point to point. It is fine for the streets to be winding and the street network varied. What is important is that the individual links in the network have clear visual characteristics, that space has a distinctive character and that important streets can be distinguished from less important ones. Signs and directions and good lighting at night are crucial elements of the relationship between city structure, sense of locality and feeling of security when walking in the city.

clear-cut territories mean safer cities

In the chapter on human senses, it was mentioned how different distances are used for various types of communication between people, and how these distances are continuously used to reinforce the character and intensity of contacts. Interacting with others and protecting our private sphere are two sides of the same coin. Just as close contact necessitates precisely defined territories, a clear articulation of private and public territories on the larger arena is an important prerequisite for social opportunities and a sense of security.

Human society is subtly organized around various social structures that define and reinforce the individual's sense of affiliation and security. A university student is part of a structure with faculties, departments, classes and study groups that provide a framework. Workplaces have divisions, departments and teams. Cities have quarters, neighborhoods, housing complexes and single dwellings. Coupled with well-known designations and signals, these structures in themselves help reinforce a sense of affiliation within the larger entity and security for the individual group, household or person.

Sibelius Park, a housing complex in Copenhagen, has cooperated with the Danish Crime Prevention Council to carefully define private, semiprivate, semipublic and public territories in the complex. Subsequent studies have shown that there is less crime and greater security than in other similar developments.[26]

Security and the ability to read a situation are reinforced when social structures are supported by clear, physical demarcations. A sign at the city limit tells us we are now entering the city. Quarters can also be marked by signs or gates, as they are known in the Chinatowns in many American cities. Neighborhoods and individual streets can be marked with signs, gates or symbolic portals, and our arrival at a housing complex can be marked with gates and welcome signs.

The marking and detailing of structure and sense of affiliation on all the levels mentioned helps strengthen the feeling of security for groups as well as individuals. People who live in the area will think: this is my city, my quarter and my street, while outsiders will think: now I am visiting others in their city, quarter or street.

In the area of crime prevention, Oscar Newman's pioneering work on "defensible space" shows a strong connection between clearly defined territorial affiliation and security. He makes a compelling argument for working consistently with clear hierarchies in city planning in order to reinforce actual and perceived security.[27]

soft transitions between private
and public space, please

Also on a small scale — particularly in connection with individual dwell-ings — clarifying territories and affiliations is crucial for contact with others and for protecting the private sphere. Whereas efforts are made to graduate and soften transitions between private and public areas by building semiprivate and semipublic transition zones, the likelihood of contact from zone to zone increases, and residents gain the opportunity to regulate contacts and protect private life. A well-proportioned transi-tion zone can keep events at a comfortable arm's length.

In the previous section soft edges and their importance for life in the city are discussed. It is emphasized that edge zones, porches and front yards can make a decisive contribution to vitalizing life in public space. These transition zones between the private and public sphere must be carefully articulated in order to clearly distinguish between what is pri-vate and what is public.

Changes in pavement, landscaping, furniture, hedges, gates and canopies can mark where public space ends and fully or semiprivate transition zones begin. Height differences, steps and staircases can also mark the transition zone, providing critical prerequisite for the impor-tant function of soft edges as the link between inside and out, between private and public. Only when territories are clearly marked can the pri-vate sphere afford the degree of protection that people need to make contact with others and contribute to life in the city.

A soft edge and clear distinctions be-tween public, semiprivate and private territories provide good opportunities to signal where you live and decorate it with your favorite flowers (Almere, the Netherlands).

pedestrian and bicycle cities as sustainability policy

The bar graph shows dramatic differences in energy consumption in cities in various parts of the world. It also shows the opportunities to achieve lower energy consumption by investing more heavily in collective traffic and bicycles, as has happened in Europe and Asia. Photo: Brisbane, Australia, is one of the cities that has not dismantled motorways along the river — yet!

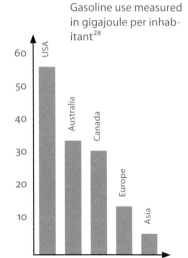

Gasoline use measured in gigajoule per inhabitant[28]

Copenhagen's bicycles save 90,000 tons of CO_2 every year. The balloon shows the volume of one ton of CO_2.

Pedestrian and bicycle traffic save a lot of space in the city. Bicycle paths have room for five times more traffic than car lanes. The sidewalk has room for 20 times more travellers than car lanes. Ten parked bicycles can easily fit into one parking space for cars.

3.3
The sustainable city

climate, resources and green city planning

There is growing interest in planning sustainable cities, and for good reason. The depletion of fossil fuels, escalating pollution, carbon emissions and the resulting threat to the climate are strong incentives for trying to increase sustainability in cities around the world.

The concept of sustainability as it applies to cities is broad, with the energy consumption and emissions of buildings being only one concern. Other key sectors are industrial production, energy supply, and water, waste and transport management. Transport is a particularly important item on the green accounting sheet because it is responsible for massive energy consumption and the resulting heavy pollution and carbon emissions. In the USA transport accounts for no less than 28% of carbon emissions.[29]

Giving higher priority to pedestrian and bicycle traffic would change the profile of the transport sector and be a significant element in overall sustainable policies.

a walking and bicycling city — an important step toward greater sustainability

Pedestrian and bicycle traffic use fewer resources and affect the environment less than any other form of transport. Users supply the energy, and this form of transport is cheap, near-silent and nonpolluting.

For a given distance the relative energy consumption ratio of biking to walking to driving a car is one to three to 60 energy units. In other words, biking will take you three times further than walking using the same amount of energy. A car consumes 60 times more energy than a bicycle and 20 times more than walking.

pedestrian and bicycle traffic takes less space

Pedestrian and bicycle traffic does not crowd city space. Pedestrians make very modest demands: two sidewalks 3.5 meters (11.5 feet) wide, or a pedestrian street seven meters (23 feet) wide can handle 20,000 people per hour. Two bike paths two meters (six feet) wide are sufficient for 10,000 bikers per hour. A two-lane, two-way street can take between 1,000 and 2,000 cars per hour (peak load).

A typical bike path can thus transport five times as many people as a car lane. And in terms of parking, there is plenty of space for ten bicycles in one ordinary parking slot. Pedestrian and bicycle traffic saves space and makes a positive contribution to green accounts by reducing particle pollution and carbon emissions.

good public transport and good city space — two sides of the same coin

Being able to walk, wait and ride comfortably are important aspects of the quality of collective transit. Quality of walking routes and comfort at stops are important issues (bus stop, San José, Costa Rica and rail commuters, Cape Town, South Africa).
Below: trolley car from Freiburg, Germany, shows the potential benefits.

Greater consideration for pedestrian and bicycle traffic can further facilitate the transition from cars to people traffic. The more people who walk and bike and the greater the distances traveled by foot or bike, the greater the rewards for total city quality and the environment. Strengthening bicycle traffic in particular provides major benefits.

developing more bicycle traffic opens promising perspectives all over the world

The topography, climate and city structure of many cities worldwide would make it simple and cheap to introduce or strengthen bicycle traffic. In addition to the many direct advantages of bike traffic in cities, bicycles will also be able to ease some of the transport burden.

For example, in the City of Copenhagen, the curbing of vehicular traffic has meant that bicyclists in 2008 accounted for 37% of commuting to and from work.[30]

In Bogotá, Columbia, pedestrian and bicycle traffic has been dramatically strengthened as a result of the overall traffic policy, showcasing the massive potential of many developing countries — with relatively modest investments — for increasing the mobility of the vast majority of their inhabitants while reducing impact on the environment.

good city space
— a crucial prerequisite for a good public transportation system

A good city landscape and good public transportation system are two sides of the same coin. The quality of journeys to and from stops and stations has a direct bearing on the efficiency and quality of public transportation systems.

The total journey from home to destination and back must be seen in its entirety. Good walking and bicycle routes and good amenities at stations are important elements — by day as well as by night — for ensuring comfort and a feeling of security.

Transport Oriented Developments

All over the world people are working on Transport Oriented Development (TOD) plans, concentrating on the interplay between pedestrian and bicycle structures and the collective traffic network.

TOD cities are typically built around light-rail systems surrounded by relatively high-density development. This structure is a prerequisite for providing a sufficient number of dwellings and workplaces with a reasonable walking and biking distance to stations. Compact TOD cities with short walking distances and good city space provide numerous other environmental advantages such as short supply lines and reduced land consumption.

Before the incursion of cars, old cities were all well-functioning TOD cities. Again Venice is a classic example. Public transport is handled by ferry buses, which ply many routes, with frequent stops creating a finely meshed transport net. No address in the city is more than 200 – 300 meters (655 – 985 feet) from the nearest ferry-bus stop, and walking along beautiful streets and squares is an important part of the total journey.

city space and social
sustainability

Social sustainability is a large and challenging concept. Part of the focus is to give various groups in society equal opportunities for accessing common city space and getting around town. Equality gets a substantial boost when people can walk and bicycle in combination with public transport. People without cars must have access to what the city has to offer and the opportunity for a daily life unrestricted by poor transport options.

Social sustainability also has a significant democratic dimension that prioritizes equal access to meet "others" in public space. A general prerequisite here is easily accessible, inviting public space that serves as an attractive setting for organized as well as informal meetings.

basic needs
– and social sustainability

Naturally there are differences in the needs and opportunities of the world's rich and poor cities. It is important to underline the idea that well-developed countries need to increase focus on social sustainability, a fundamental to creating a well-functioning and attractive city for everyone.

The problems are considerably more urgent in low-income urban societies, because the gap between rich and poor is so vast, with widespread poverty limiting the opportunities of marginalized population groups. Tackling the problems of these societies requires new resource priorities, visionary city policies and capable leadership like that demonstrated in Bogotá Colombia, in the period around the year 2000.

lively cities and social
sustainability

The principles underlying the creation of a lively city also support plans for social sustainability. The lively city tries to counter the trend for people to withdraw into gated communities and promotes the idea of a city that is accessible and attractive to all groups in society. The city is seen as serving a democratic function where people encounter social diversity and gain a greater understanding of each other by sharing the same city space. The concept of sustainability also implies thinking about coming generations. They too must be considered as communities around the world become increasingly urbanized. The city must be inclusive and there must be room for everyone.

For cities to achieve social sustainability, attempts must reach far beyond physical structures. If cities are to function efforts must focus on all aspects from the physical environment and social institutions to the less obvious cultural aspects that have great significance on how we perceive individual quarters and entire city societies.

a sedentary life behind steering wheel and computer screen

An inactive life behind steering wheel and computer screen quickly turn into a serious health problem. In recent years obesity has become an epedemic in countries where natural exercise is not part of the daily pattern of activity.

Number of obese in the adult part of the population (≥ 15 years)[31]

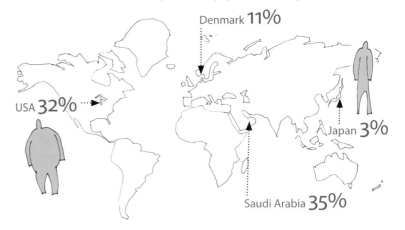

Denmark **11%**

USA **32%**

Japan **3%**

Saudi Arabia **35%**

Where walking and biking are not part of the daily program, people have to run for their lives in their lunch breaks. Another option: Park'n Sweat facilities like this one, seven stories of parking with a two-storey fitness center on top (Atlanta, Georgia).

good city space — a valuable contribution to health policy

The interplay between health and city planning is a comprehensive topic. In this section discussion will be limited to health and health policy seen in relation to work on the human dimension of city planning.

a sedentary life behind steering wheel and computer screen

Numerous changes in society in the economically developed world have led to new health policy challenges. Sedentary work has largely replaced the manual labor of the past, cars have increasingly become the dominant mode of transport, and simple activities such as climbing stairs are increasingly replaced by riding on escalators and elevators instead. If we add that much of our time at home is spent in an easy chair passively watching TV, we have a model in which many people do not have natural opportunities for using their bodies and energy on a daily basis. Poor eating habits, overeating and eating fat-saturated foods often reinforce the problem.

Country after country admits that the problem is epidemic in proportion. Following the history of the obesity epidemic in the USA makes for dramatic reading.

Year for year the problem has spread from state to state, while the situation in each state gradually worsens. The number of people classified as overweight in the USA has been relatively constant since the 1960s, but the number of obese people has risen sharply. Obesity is defined as people with a BMI over 30, the standard used by WHO and other organizations. In the 1970s one in ten Americans was obese. In the period 2000 – 2007 the rate has risen to one in three.[32]

The pattern for children is particular worrying, with the number of overweight children ages 6 to 11 having doubled in the past three decades from 1980 to 2006. The number has tripled for youth ages 12 to 19.[33]

In the past ten years these lifestyle-related health problems have spread quickly to other parts of the world with corresponding economies and societies. The problem of obesity is extensive in Canada, Australia and New Zealand and growing rapidly in other areas such as Central America, Europe and the Middle East. In the UK about a quarter of the adult population is obese, in Mexico about a third, and one-third of the population in Saudi Arabia is obese.[34]

The price of the loss of exercise as part of a daily pattern of activity is high: a decrease in quality of life, a dramatic rise in health costs and a shorter lifespan.

exercise by choice

Providing opportunities for exercise and self-expression is a logical and valuable answer to the new challenges (winter skating on Copenhagen square; skateboarding in New York; students compensating for their commuting in cars, University of Miami; and street scenes from China).

exercise as a cause, a choice
and a business opportunity

The solution to these new challenges is that the individual must seek physical challenges and daily exercise, which are no longer an integral part of daily life. In Denmark the most popular form of sport in 2008 was "running" and in their free time people jogging flock to paths and parks where they make a valuable contribution to the activity level in cities. Other people choose organized sport or fitness centers for their exercise and quality of life boost. Many others have purchased their own fitness equipment and bike, step and run at home. Exercise has become a widespread and important daily activity, as well as a major business.

This entire development is logical and appropriate for the individual and for society, but individual and private solutions also have their limitations.

Voluntary exercise requires time, determination and willpower. Organized options and equipment also cost money. Some social groups and age groups can handle the challenges, but many people do not have the time, money or energy, and there are often periods during life where people do not get as much exercise as they should. "Fitness freaks" are often healthy and physically active, while the problems of too little exercise are widespread among children and seniors and to a surprisingly high extent even our youth.

exercise as a natural part of
daily life

In the face of new and old challenges, one important aspect of overall health policy is near to hand. Why not introduce a broad, carefully conceived invitation to people to walk and bicycle as much as possible in connection with their daily activities? Naturally, invitations must comprise physical infrastructure in the form of quality walking and bicycling routes, coupled with an information campaign to let people know about the advantages and opportunities that await when they use their own personal energy supply for transport.

A number of cities, including Copenhagen and Melbourne, have recently introduced general objectives that more closely define the requirement of whole-hearted invitations to walk and bicycle as much as possible in existing and new urban areas. In several cities such as New York, Sydney and Mexico City work is ongoing to develop infrastructure and city culture so that pedestrian and bicycle traffic can occupy a prominent place in the daily pattern.

These cities have prioritized improvements, upgrading pedestrian networks with broader sidewalks, laying better surfaces, planting shade trees, removing unnecessary sidewalk interruptions and improving street crossings. The goal is to make it simple, uncomplicated and safe to walk any time of day or night. And it should also be a pleasure with beautiful space, good city furniture, fine details and good lighting.

For bicyclists in the years following the millennium in 2000, thousands of kilometers of good bicycle routes and paths have been laid out all over the world, offering uncomplicated, fast and safe travel through cities.

When walking and bicycling are a natural part of the daily pattern of activity, there is positive spin-off for the life quality and well-being of the individual — and even greater benefits to society.

In new urban areas adopting a policy of inviting people to walk and bicycle regularly might sound like an obvious and feasible prospect, but if the invitation is to mean anything, plenty of innovative thinking and new planning processes will be required. After all, urban planners worldwide have been accustomed to planning exclusively for car traffic for decades now.

Convincing invitations to walk and bike will require a change in planning culture. Plans for new cities must start by designing the shortest, most attractive walking and biking connections and then address the other transport needs. This planning priority will result in new city quarters that are more compact with smaller space dimensions. In other words, it will be far more attractive to live, work and move about in these neighborhoods than in the city quarters built to today's conventional standards. Life must come before space, which in turn must come before buildings.

"An apple a day keeps the doctor away," is a health slogan that has been around a long time. Today's advice for a healthier life is to walk 10,000 steps a day. If old and new city areas are laid out to invite pedestrian traffic or a combination of walking and biking traffic that can easily meet daily transportation needs, many health problems could be reduced and both life quality and city quality improved.[35]

In old cities almost all traffic was by foot. Walking was the way to get around, the way to experience society and people on a daily basis. City space was meeting place, market place and movement space between the various functions of the city. The common denominator was travel by foot.

In Venice it is easy to walk 10,000, 15,000 or even 20,000 steps on an ordinary day. You don't think of it as any great distance because of the wealth of impressions gained on route and the beautiful city space. You just walk.

city life, safety, sustainability and health as an integrated city policy!

A look back at the discussions in this chapter about lively, safe, sustainable and healthy cities underscores the interconnectedness of the issues and the enormous opportunities that increased concern for pedestrians, bicyclists and city life in general can mean for all four areas.

A single city policy change will strengthen city quality and key social objectives. In addition to other benefits, a stronger invitation to walk and bicycle in cities can be made quickly and cheaply. It would be visible, have major signal value and be a policy for all the users of the city.

However, actions must match words, and good physical frameworks must be established. And most important of all, we must work whole-heartedly to invite people to walk and bicycle in cities as part of their everyday routine. Invitation is the key word and in this connection city quality on the small scale — at eye level — is crucial.

A vital element in overall health policy should be for walking and bicycling in cities to be an obvious option. Benefits are substantial for increasing life quality and reducing health-care costs.

4

The city
at eye level

4.1
The battle for quality is on the small scale

the city at eye level — the most important scale for city planning

In many cities, particularly those in developing countries, a great deal of pedestrian traffic is generated by nessisity. In other parts of the world, the number of pedestrians depends entirely on the extent to which people are invited to walk.

City quality is important regardless of whether foot traffic is a question of necessity or invitation. Good city quality at eye level should be considered a basic human right wherever people go in cities.

It is on the small scale, in the 5 km/h (3 mph) urban landscape, that people encounter the city close up. It is here that the individual out walking has time to enjoy quality — or suffers from its lack.

Regardless of planning ideologies and economic prerequisites, careful management of the human dimension in all types of cities and urban areas should be a universal requirement.

walking, standing, sitting, listening and talking
— a good place to start

The following is an overview of the principles for human dimension planning in cities. The starting point is simple: universal human activities. Cities must provide good conditions for people to walk, stand, sit, watch, listen and talk.

If these basic activities, which are tied to the human sensory and motor apparatus, can take place under good conditions, these and related activities will be able to unfold in all possible combinations in the human landscape. Of all the city planning tools available, attention to this small scale is the most important.

If the living room in a home does not work for its owner on a daily basis, a carefully planned city or housing complex will be of little comfort. In contrast, the quality of a dwelling and city space at eye level can in itself be decisive to everyday quality of life despite deficiencies in other planning areas.

Consideration for people's direct senses is crucial to whether they can walk, sit, listen and talk inside buildings, in the neighborhood or in town. The battle for quality is on the small scale.

4.2
Good cities for walking

life happens on foot

It is a big day when at about one year of age a child takes its first step. The child's eye level moves from the vantage point of the crawler (about 30 cm/1 foot) above the floor to about 80 cm/2.6 feet.

The little walker can see much more and move faster. From now on everything in the child's world — field of vision, perspective, overview, pace, flexibility and opportunities — will move on a higher, faster plane. All of life's important moments will hereafter be experienced on foot at standing and walking pace.

While walking is basically a linear movement that brings the walker from place to place, it is also much more. Walkers can effortlessly stop underway to change direction, maneuver, speed up or slow down or switch to a different type of activity such as standing, sitting, running, dancing, climbing or lying down.

Life takes place by foot (Lucca, Italy; Amman, Jordan; and Marrakesh, Morocco).

the city at eye level   119

walking with a purpose — and as a beginning

There is more to walking than walking.

walking with a purpose — and as beginning

A city walk illustrates its many variations: the quick goal-oriented walk from A to B, the slow stroll to enjoy city life or a sunset, children's zig-zagging, and senior citizens' determined walk to get fresh air and exercise or do an errand. Regardless of the purpose, a walk in city space is a "forum" for the social activities that take place along the way as an integral part of pedestrian activities. Heads move from side to side, walkers turn or stop to see everything, or to greet or talk with others. Walking is a form of transport, but it is also a potential beginning or an occasion for many other activities.

how fast?

Many factors impact on walking speed: the quality of the route, the surface, the strength of the crowd, and the age and mobility of the walker. The design of the space also plays a role. Pedestrians usually walk faster on street that invite linear movement, while their pace falls while traversing squares. It is almost like water, which flows rapidly along riverbeds but moves more slowly in lakes. Weather is another factor. People move more quickly when it is raining, windy or cold.

On Copenhagen's main walking street, Strøget, pedestrian traffic on cold winter days is 35% faster than on good summer days. In summer there are many pedestrians in the city promenading and enjoying the process, while pedestrian traffic in winter is considerably more targeted. When it's cold, people walk for warmth. On average the walking speed in summer is 14.2 min per km/23 min per mile, corresponding to 4.2 km per hour/2.6 mph. Corresponding winter walking speeds are 10.3 min per km/16.6 min per mile corresponding to 5.8 km per hour/3.6 mph.[1]

A walk of 450 m/0.3 mile takes about five minutes, while a walk of 900 m/0.6 mile will take about 10 minutes at 5.4 km per hour/3.4 mph. Naturally, these time estimates are only valid if the area is uncrowded and people can walk without obstacles or breaks.

An acceptable walking distance is a relatively fluid concept. Some people happily walk many kilometers/miles, while even short walks are difficult for old people, the disabled and children. Walks of 500 m/0.3 miles are mentioned frequently as a distance most people are willing to walk. However, an acceptable distance also depends on the quality of the route. If the pavement is good quality and the route interesting, a considerably longer walk is often acceptable. Conversely, the desire to walk drops drastically if the route is uninteresting and thus feels tiring. In that case a walk of only 200 or 300 m/0.12 to 0.18 mile will seem like a long way, even if it only takes less than five minutes on foot.[2]

A distance of 500 m/0.3 mile as an approximate goal for acceptable walks is supported by the size of city centers. By far the majority of city centers are about one km²/0.39 sq mile, corresponding to an area of 1x1 km/0.6 x 0.6 mile. This means that a walk of a kilometer or less will bring the pedestrians around to most of the functions in the city.

Huge cities like London and New York have corresponding patterns, as they are divided into numerous centers and districts. The magic one km² center size can certainly be found in these cities. The acceptable walking distance does not change just because the city is larger.

An important prerequisite for a comfortable and pleasurable walk is room to walk relatively freely and unhampered, without having to weave in and out and without being pushed and shoved by others. Children, older people and people with disabilities have special requirements for being able to walk unhindered. People pushing strollers, shopping carts and walkers also need plenty of room for walking. Groups of young people are typically the most tolerant about moving about in crowds.

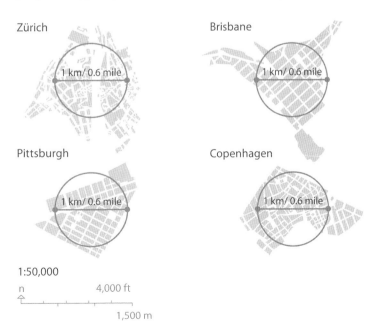

Zürich

Brisbane

Pittsburgh

Copenhagen

1:50,000

n

4,000 ft

1,500 m

Most city centers measure one square km/0.39 square mile, which enables pedestrians to reach all important city functions by walking one kilometer/ 0.6 mile or less.

This street sign in Poland discreetly recommends that people keep their arms close to their sides.

The high priority given to car traffic and parking have created unreasonable conditions for pedestrians all over the world.
Enough space for walking is important to all groups of pedestrians, but especially children, the elderly and the disabled.

If we look at photographs from 100 years ago, pedestrians are often shown moving freely and unimpeded in every direction. Cities were still primarily the province of pedestrians, with horse-drawn carriages and trolleys and a few cars merely as visitors.

In step with the car invasion, pedestrians were first pushed up along building façades and then increasingly squeezed together on shrinking sidewalks. Crowded sidewalks are unacceptable and a problem worldwide.

Studies of urban streets in London, New York and Sydney illustrate the problems of narrow sidewalks for large crowds of pedestrians on streets where most of the area is designed for car traffic, despite the fact that the number of drivers is far lower than the number of pedestrians crowded together on the sidewalk.[3]

The pedestrian traffic on sidewalks moves in columns that are pushed and shoved, and everyone must move at the speed dictated by the pedestrian stream. The elderly, the disabled and children cannot possibly keep up.

Various limits are suggested for what is considered an acceptable amount of space for pedestrian traffic, depending on context. Based on studies in New York, William H. Whyte proposes up to 23 pedestrians per minute per meter/three feet on the sidewalk. Studies in Copenhagen propose 13 pedestrians per minute per meter/three feet of sidewalk, if the limit for unacceptable crowding on sidewalks is to be avoided.[4]

slalom for pedestrians

If walking is to be comfortable, including acceptable distance and pace, there has to be room to walk without too many interruptions and obstacles. These qualities are often offered in dedicated pedestrian areas, but seldom on sidewalks on city streets. On the contrary, it is impressive to note how many obstacles and difficulties have been incorporated into pedestrian landscapes over the years. Traffic signs, lampposts, parking meters and all types of technical control units are systematically placed on sidewalks in order "not to be in the way." Cars parked on or partially on sidewalks, thoughtlessly parked bicycles and undisciplined street displays complete the picture of a pedestrian landscape where pedestrians have to maneuver like skiers down a slalom course in order to move along sidewalks that are too narrow in the first place.

irritating detours and meaning-less interruptions

Walking in urban landscapes can present many other petty annoyances and difficulties. One is pedestrian fences intended to keep walkers confined to crowded sidewalks. Barriers erected on pavements at intersections to keep pedestrians away from corners extend some way down the street, causing more detours and annoyance

Interruptions in sidewalks to provide cars with uncomplicated access to garages, driveways, delivery gates and gas stations have gradually become a natural part of the street scene in car-dominated cities. On

When walking resembles an obstacle course (Sydney, Australia, and Middlesbrough, UK).

Many cities have consistently allowed entrances, garages and side streets to interrupt sidewalks. However, cars should yield on side streets, allowing pedestrians and bicycles to continue on without interruption (Regent Street, London, and standard traffic solution in Copenhagen).

Regent Street in London, 45 – 50,000 pedestrians daily force their way through 13 unnecessary sidewalk interruptions,[5] and in Adelaide, South Australia, streets in the city center offer pedestrians no fewer than 330 unnecessary sidewalk interruptions[6]

In addition to these meaningless interruptions that force pedestrians, wheelchairs and strollers up and down curbs at garages and gates, there are many unmotivated interruptions where small streets run into larger ones. In almost all of the situations mentioned, the sidewalk should be led unbroken through entrance ways and side streets as part of a general policy of inviting rather than discouraging pedestrian traffic.

walking in crowds and waiting forever

The combination of inadequate space and annoyances large and small is supplemented by endless waiting time at stoplights at city intersections. Pedestrians are typically given low priority and thus face long waits at red lights followed by short green-light periods. The green light often only lasts seconds before being replaced by blinking red signals meaning that it is now time to run to avoid delaying the traffic.

In many places, particularly in the UK and other areas inspired by British traffic planning, crossing the streets is not a basic human right but rather something pedestrians have to apply for by pushing a button at intersections. Sometimes they even have to press three times to make it through the maze at complicated intersections. In these cities any thought of being able to walk 450 meters/1,476 feet in five minutes is a fantasy.

The center of Sydney has many pedestrians, as well as many intersections, many stoplights, many pushbuttons and long periods of waiting. Here pedestrians can easily spend half of the total walking time waiting for the "walk" signal.[7]

Waits of up to 15%, 25% or even 50% of a walk are common on many traffic streets in cities around the world.

By comparison, the waiting time on a one-kilometer/0.6 mile walk on Copenhagen's main walking street, Strøget, is only 0 – 3% of walking time. A goal-oriented walk through the city via Strøget can be done in 12 minutes, but many people spend far more time because the walk is so interesting.[8]

Another special walking phenomenon has been noted on sidewalks where crossroads streets and light signals cause pedestrians to stop frequently. Pedestrians move in clumps and therefore always in crowds, even at times when there isn't much pedestrian traffic.

Every time the pedestrian stream meets a red light the pedestrians stop, and the slightly slower walkers have time to catch up with the main field, after which everyone is once again amalgamated into a clump. When the light turns green, the clump moves forward again, but disperses slightly before the next stoplight, where everyone is gathered once again. Between clumps, the sidewalk is typically almost devoid of people.

Crossing the street should be a human right rather than something one must apply for (push button in Australia and friendly information in China).

Architects dislike detours as much as anyone else (School of Architecture, Copenhagen, Denmark).

People's ability to find the shortest route can be traced in the snow on city squares and on the lawns of universities (City Hall Square, Copenhagen, Denmark, and Harvard University, Cambridge, Massachusetts).

direct lines of walking, please

Urbanites all over the world are highly energy conscious when it comes to saving their own energy when walking. They cross streets where it is most natural for them, avoid detours, obstacles, stairs and steps, and prefer direct lines of walking everywhere.

When pedestrians can see the object of a walk, they rechart a course along the shortest line. Their pleasure from direct walks can be seen clearly in city squares, by their footsteps after a snowfall and on countless tramped paths worn across lawns and landscapes the world over.

Walking directly to your destination is a natural response, often in an unfortunate and almost comic conflict with architects' rulers and the resulting right-angled urban projects. These right-angled design projects look neat and proper until the corners, lawns and squares are trodden on in every direction.

It is often easy to foresee the preferred lines of walking and to incorporate them to a reasonable extent in the design of complexes and landscaping. Preferred lines often inspire fascinating patterns and shapes.

physical distance and perceived distance

About 500 meters/1,640 feet is a distance most pedestrians find acceptable. This is not an absolute truth, however, because what is acceptable will always be a combination of distance and the quality of the route. If comfort is low, the walk will be short, while if the route is interesting, rich in experience and comfortable, pedestrians forget the distance and enjoy experiences as they happen.

walk psychology

The "tiring length perspective" describes the situation in which the pedestrian can see the whole route at a glance before even starting out. The road is straight and seemingly endless, with no promise of interesting experiences along the way. The prospect is tiring before the walk is even begun.

In contrast, the route can be divided into manageable segments, where people can walk from square to square, which naturally breaks up the walk, or along a street that winds enticingly, inviting the pedestrian from one section to the next. A winding street does not have to twist much to prevent the walker seeing very far down the street, but is constantly walking towards corners and twists, where new vistas open.

Below right: even a long walk feels short along a curved road with plenty to see (Cartagena, Colombia). Below left: conversely, a walk can seem endless when the route has a long tiring perspective devoid of encouragement along the way (Ørestad, Copenhagen).

stairs and steps, no thanks

Walking up stairs is harder than walking on a flat surface, and we avoid stairs whenever we can. And for many groups in society stairs are a direct barrier.

Right: If we can see the staircase all the way to the top, we find the climb all the more tiring.

Piles on stairs to be carried up when convenient tell their own story about stairs as actual and psychological barriers.

Copenhagen's main pedestrian street, Strøget, is a good kilometer/0.6 mile long and runs almost directly from one end of the city center to the other. Countless twists and turns along the way keep the spaces closed up and interesting. Four squares further divide the route and make walking the length of the city center psychologically manageable. We walk from square to square, and the many twists and turns make the trip interesting and unpredictable. Under these circumstances a walk of one kilometer/0.6 mile or more is no problem.

interesting things to see
at eye level, please

Street patterns, the design of space, rich detail and intense experiences influence the quality of pedestrian routes and pleasure in walking. The city's "edges" also play a role. We have plenty of time to look as we walk, and the quality of the ground floor façades we pass close by at eye level, is particularly important to the quality of the tour. The section on lively cities proscribes "small units and many doors" for streets frequented by pedestrians.

narrow units, many details and
vertical façade rhythms, please

The principle of narrow units and many experiences is also important along pedestrian routes that don't have shops and stalls. Front doors, building details, landscaping and greenery in front of housing, offices and institutions can make a valuable contribution to interesting experiences on walks.

If buildings also have a primarily vertical façade expression, walks seem shorter and more manageable, whereas buildings with powerful horizontal lines underscore and reinforce distance.

stairs and steps, no thanks

Stairs and steps are another area that clearly illustrate pedestrians' major interest in saving energy. Horizontal movements are no big problem. If the telephone rings in a neighboring room, we just get up and answer it. However, if the telephone rings on another floor, we shout to ask if someone else will answer it. Going up and down stairs and steps requires new movements, more muscle power, and walking rhythm has to be changed to climbing rhythm. These factors make it more difficult to go up and down than to move on the same plane, or alternatively, to be transported mechanically up and down. At metro stations, in airports and department stores, people stand in line to take the escalator, while staircases next to them are almost empty. Shopping malls and department stores built in several stories rely on escalators and elevators to move people from floor to floor. If the transport breaks down, people go home!

stairs as a physical
and psychological barrier

It is interesting to study daily life in multistory housing. In almost all cases, the bulk of activity takes place on the ground floor. Once you have entered the living room, you naturally tend to wait before going upstairs again. Children bring their toys down into the living room, where they

ramps rather than stairs, thanks

If we have a choice between a ramp and stairs, we almost always choose the ramp.
Right: Marathon preparation in Venice means ramps instead of stairs.

Shoppers have a choice of ramps, stairs and escalators at this shopping center in Beijing, China.

play with them all day until their parents take them back up again at bedtime. The lower floors are almost always more well-worn than the upper ones. Second- or third-floor rooms are almost always used less than those on the ground floor, and roof terraces are used far less than outside space with direct access without climbing stairs. The heaps gathered on the bottom steps waiting to be taken upstairs speak volumes about the physical and psychological problems related to internal stairs.

applied stair psychology

Stairs and steps definitely represent a genuine physical and psychological challenge for pedestrians. If possible pedestrians certainly will avoid them. However, like street length, staircases can also be disguised to

*Staircases as sculpture and city space for moving and staying.
(Piazza di Spagna, Rome, Italy).*

make the trip seem more doable. If at the foot of a five-story building we could see the entire staircase with its seemingly endless steps, most people would find it impossible to crawl to the top, unless their lives were at stake. In situations like these it is interesting to see the widespread use of elementary "staircase psychology."

Staircases are angled to wind from landing to landing, dividing the climb into shorter segments. It is like moving from "square" to "square," and the climber never gets the chance to see the entire course of stairs in its exhausting length. That way we are enticed into the building, even if we have to climb. Even when the enticement is utterly convincing, it is the elevator that is the most used if there is one. Naturally staircase psychology is also used successfully in public space, where examples like the Spanish Steps in Rome demonstrate that a climb can be beautifully combined with interesting experiences.

With regard to visions of lovely urban space that invite people to walk as much as possible, the conclusion is actually very simple. Stairs and steps are genuine obstacles — in principle to be avoided wherever possible. When a necessity in the pedestrian landscape, stairs and steps must have comfortable dimensions, and visual interest and staircase psychology must be used purposefully. Ramps or elevators are established for rolling pedestrian traffic and people with reduced mobility as a matter of course.

ramps rather than stairs

If we consider situations where pedestrians are free to choose between ramps and stairs, we see that they clearly prefer ramps. Walking rhythm can be maintained if height differences are evened out by allowing the terrain to rise and fall slightly or by using ramps. Children, the disabled and rolling pedestrian traffic can also complete their walk without interruptions. Ramps are not always as full of character as stairs and steps, but they are generally preferred.

pedestrian underpasses and bridges as a last resort

In the early years of the automobile invasion, from the 1950s to the 1970s, road engineering focused uncritically on increasing capacity on the roads and preventing accidents to pedestrians. The solution to both problems was often to segregate traffic and lead pedestrians under or over roads by means of pedestrian underpasses and bridges. This meant subjecting pedestrians to stairs on either side of the crossing. Planners quickly learned that pedestrian underpasses and bridges were exceedingly unpopular and only worked if tall fences were also built along the roads, so that pedestrians literally had no other way out. This still did not solve the problem of strollers, wheelchairs and bicycles, however.

Pedestrian underpass systems had the additional disadvantage of being dark and dank, and people generally feel insecure if they are unable to see very far ahead. In short, the often expensive pedestrian underpasses and bridges were in conflict with the basic premises for

pedestrian bridges

Pedestrian overpasses are used as a last resort and only function as intended if pedestrians are physically prevented from crossing the street at grade.
Right: in Japanese cities the overpasses are intertwined into larger systems. Level of difficulty: great. Chances of interesting promenades: small (Sendai, Japan).

good pedestrian landscapes. Seen in the perspective of current visions of inviting people to walk and bicycle more in cities, clearly pedestrian underpasses and bridges can only be solutions in those special cases where major highways must be crossed. Solutions must be found for all other roads and streets that allow pedestrians and bicycles to stay on street level and cross with dignity. An integrated traffic model will also make city streets friendlier and safer as cars will have to move more slowly and stop more often.

Today the world is full of abandoned pedestrian underpasses and bridges. They belong to a certain time and a certain philosophy.

uneven cobblestone and flat flagstone

Naturally pavements play an important role in pedestrian comfort. In future the quality of pavement and surfaces will be particularly impor-

Cobblestones are full of character but not exactly pedestrian friendly.

For many years pedestrians were forced to use tunnels to reach the main railway station in Zurich, Switzerland. The tunnels have now been replaced by pedestrian crossings at street level.

tant in a world with more senior citizens and pedestrians with reduced mobility, more rolling pedestrian traffic and more people wanting to take children to the city. It is desirable for surfaces to be even and non slip. Traditional cobblestones and broken natural slate stones are full of visual character, but seldom live up to modern requirements. In places where the character of the old cobblestones has to be maintained, bands of flat granite have to be added to enable wheelchairs, strollers, small children, senior citizens and women in high heels to move in relative comfort. This type of pavement, combining old with new, is used in many cities and can be designed as elegant floors for public space, while paying history its due.

around the clock all year round, please

As far as possible, a good city for walking must function all year round, day and night. In winter it is important that snow and ice are cleared, and, to use the Copenhagen model as an example, pedestrian areas and bicycle paths should be cleared before roads for car traffic. On cold days when pavements are icy, pedestrians have a far greater risk of injury than do car drivers, who typically drive more slowly and carefully. In all parts of the world and in all seasons, ensuring dry nonslip surfaces for pedestrians is an important part of whole-hearted invitations to walk in cities.

Lighting is crucial once night falls. Good lighting on people and faces and reasonable lighting for façades, niches and corners is needed along the most important pedestrian routes to strengthen the real and the experienced sense of security, and sufficient light is needed on pavements, surfaces and steps so that pedestrians can maneuver safely.

Please walk — around the clock all year round.

poor cities — rich cities

Two main groups of activities take place in city space: moving activities and stationary activities.

Like moving activities, stationary activities also cover a wide spectrum. The extent and character of the activities depend greatly on the surrounding culture and economic level. In many cities in economically developing countries, most activities are dictated by necessity. Every type of activity takes place in public space, and the pressure of external necessity means that the quality of city space has no great bearing on city life.

In the more economically developed part of the world, city life, particularly stationary activities, is far more influenced by optional activities. People walk, stand and sit where the quality of city space invites them to do so.

Quality is essential to city life in more prosperous cities. However, there are good reasons for accommodating and showing concern for people all over the world, whatever the economic resources.

In the following, requirements for good cities for staying are discussed, with invitations and city quality as the starting point.

the necessary and optional activities

Stationary activities can be described very simply on a scale according to degree of necessity. On one end of the scale we find the necessary activities that are not particularly dependent on city quality: street trade, cleaning and maintenance. Goods are carried back and forth, and people wait patiently at intersections and bus stops. On the other end of the scale are the optional, recreational staying activities, including the many stays on benches and café chairs so that people can survey the city and follow city life. Here the quality of the situation, weather and site are decisive.

a good city can be recognized by the many people not walking

City quality is so crucial for optional activities that the extent of staying activities can often be used as a measuring stick for the quality of the city as well as of its space. Many pedestrians in a city are not necessarily an indication of good city quality — many people walking around can often be a sign of insufficient transit options or long distances between the various functions in the city. Conversely, it can be claimed that a city in which many people are not walking often indicates good city quality. In a city like Rome, it is the large number of people standing or sitting

Staying activities are very different from one part of the world to another. In developing countries almost all staying activities in cities are dictated by necessity, while they are largely recreational and by choice in more prosperous countries (Yogyakarta, Indonesia, and Rome, Italy).

in squares rather than walking that is conspicuous. And it's not due to necessity but rather that the city quality is so inviting. It is hard to keep moving in city space with so many temptations to stay. In contrast are many new quarters and complexes that many people walk through but rarely stop or stay in.

standing

Standing is typically a short-term activity. There are limits to how long a person can stand comfortably, and quality requirements for the site are correspondingly minimal. The pedestrian can always stop a moment to take a quick look at what is happening. Or look in a window, or listen

edge effect

Known as the edge effect, the edges of public space hold a magnetic attraction for people. Here our senses can master the space, we are facing what is happening and our backs are covered (examples from New Zealand, USA, Australia and China).

to street musicians, greet friends or just take a short break. These brief stops typically take place spontaneously in city space without any special regard for location and comfort. The pedestrian stops and stands if there is a problem or if a good offer beckons.

edge effect

The situation is dramatically different if pedestrians need to stop for a longer time. Then they need to find a good place to stand. If they're not sure just how long they'll be there, for example, if they're waiting for someone or something, they carefully seek out a good place to be.

Wherever people stay for a while, they seek out places along the edges of space, this phenomenon can be defined as the "edge effect." When we stand at the edge, we are not in the way of pedestrian traffic, and we can stay rather quietly and discreetly. Edge placement provides a number of important benefits: space in front to watch everything, your back covered so that no surprises will come from behind, and often good physical and psychological support. We can stand in niches and recesses and lean up against a wall. Local climate is often better at the edges of city space because the person is protected from the elements to some degree. This is a good place to be.

The preference for staying at the edges of space is closely tied to our senses and social contact norms. The principle of good edge placement can be traced back to our caveman ancestors. They sat with their backs against the back wall of their caves with the world in front of them. More recently we can see the phenomenon in a ballroom, where people spend their time between dances as "wall flowers" along the walls. And when we're at home, we can often be found in the living room's corner sofa.

Placement along edges is extra important in city space where longer stays take place among strangers, because no one wants to signal that they are waiting alone. If we stand along the façade, at least we have something to support us.

City space without edges provides poor conditions for staying. It is common to find city space that "sways freely" in a larger space, typically surrounded by heavy traffic and with no contact with the surrounding façades. Direct contact with buildings on just one of the four sides of a square will often significantly enhance staying activities, providing an opportunity to stage active functions directly on to the square. Activities on the ground floors can help change the square from a walk-through square to a staying square.

What many empty city spaces in new cities and complexes have in common is that no careful work was done to provide active edges and staying opportunities. There is literally no reason for anyone to stay there.

piano effect or the pleasure of finding support

Studies of the behavior of people at receptions provide important information about good places for staying. One cardinal rule is that guests,

something to hold on to

Like all humans, children, seniors, the clergy and laymen need practical and psychological support while in city space (examples from Italy, Denmark and Guatemala).

particularly early arrivals, spontaneously seek out places to stand along the walls. Another characteristic behavior is the "piano effect" that leads guests to find furniture, corners, columns or niches within the edge zone that will provide support for staying and help to define the place as a specially well-defined place rather than just a place along the wall. With a glass in one hand, guests have an activity. With the wall at their back, they find the place unpretentious and safe, and with a nearby piano or column they are not alone but in good company and in charge of the situation.

Façade details, inventory and equipment also provide support points for staying in the edge zones of public space. Bollards, which we know from the Piazza Del Campo in Siena, are a good example of the support function for city life. A good deal of all the activities in the Campo take place near, around or leaning on one of these bollards. On a good day in Siena it is impossible to find a bollard that hasn't already been claimed for support. Imagine what would happen if all the bollards in Siena were suddenly removed: a great deal of the activities at this city arena would be homeless, which would most probably reduce the activity level drastically.

Urban edges are potentially popular staying zones, but it is important to stress that the most attractive staying zones are those where edge zones and good façade details work together. Not all façades invite staying. Closed, smooth façades devoid of detail have the opposite effect, in fact, signaling: "Please move on."

niche effect or the pleasure of being almost present

Urban edges and façades details with columns, steps and niches must always be considered in context. It is not enough for city space to have edges: these edges must offer details that signal "please stop here and make yourself comfortable."

Among the city's façade elements, "caves" and niches take top billing as particularly attractive places for staying. It is easy to find support in a niche: there is something to lean on, protection against wind and weather, and a good view of what is going on. A key attraction is the opportunity a niche offers someone to make only a partial public appearance. In a niche, the individual has the option of pulling back and becoming almost invisible, as well as being able to move out again if something exciting beckons.

cities for staying have rough façades and good support points

The previous section mentioned the psychology of walking trips and stairs. This section on staying activities in the city offers similar observations about senses and behavior, which provide the basis for recommendations about how to reinforce staying opportunities in the city. Quite simply, good cities for staying have rough façades and good support points. In contrast, cities without edges or with smooth building façades devoid of detail have little to offer in terms of "staying psychology."

cities for staying have richly detailed façades

Niches and openings in city walls are particularly popular for staying (examples from Spain, Portugal, Mexico and Canada).

sitting

People needing to stay for any length of time in city space find it tiring to stand and will look about for somewhere to sit. The longer the envisaged stay, the more carefully the individual will choose the place to sit. The best places almost always combine many advantages and few disadvantages.

where is the attractive seating?

A four-point scale was developed to assess seating quality in conjunction with a 1990 study of city quality in the center of Stockholm.[9] In short, general requirements for a good place to sit are a pleasant microclimate, good placement preferably at the edge of the space with your back covered, a good view, an appropriately low noise level to allow conversation, and no pollution. And of course: the view. If the place offers special attractions such as water, trees, flowers, fine space, good architecture and art works, the individual wants a good view of them. At the same time, the individual wants a good view of the life and people at the site.

Architecture students also like to stay along irregular façades (Aberdeen, Scotland).

Naturally, attractive views are dependent on the opportunities at the site, but the view of city life and people has special status as main attraction. When local climate, placement, protection and view join forces, the seating place provides the best of all worlds. The individual thinks "This is a good place to be, and I can be here for a long time."

Not unexpectedly, the Stockholm studies showed a clear connection between the quality of the city's seating and the use of the individual locations. Seating with little to offer was seldom used, 7 – 12% occupied, while benches with many qualities were used often and claimed an occupation percentage from 61 – 72%. The study, which was conducted on summer days with good weather also showed that city benches are rarely occupied.

There are almost always a certain number of vacant seats in public bench landscapes, because someone has just moved away, people are rather spread out or because an arm's length distance is being maintained for certain individuals or groups.

For the most popular "bench with a view" at Sergelstorget in Stockholm, the waiting time around noon between vacant seating was 22 seconds. However, despite the demand for the good seats, they only had a 70% occupancy rate. Vacant seats enhance the impression of physical and psychological comfort on the benches. People want to sit near other people, but not too close.[10]

primary and secondary seating

The comfort of seating influences the choice of seating and length of stay. A sufficient and varied selection of seating in the city can be established with a combination of primary and secondary seating. Primary seating consists of actual furniture with backs and arms: city benches, freestanding chairs and café chairs. In all cases the backs and arms of the seating will only contribute to comfort if people want to stay for a while or for the senior citizens who need support while seated and when sit-

Trees, benches and litter bins evenly distributed through the square offer neither comfortable places to stay nor a pleasant visual environment (Cordoba, Spain).

ting and getting up again. The seating design also impacts on comfort, of course, as do the materials, insulation and water-repellent properties of the seats.

In addition to comfortable, well-situated primary seating, many secondary seating options are often needed, places where people can more informally and spontaneously sit to rest or look around. A great variety of objects can be used to sit on: pedestals, steps, stones, bollards, monuments, fountains or the city floor itself. On days when seating is in high demand, secondary seating can make a valuable contribution to the city's total seating selection. Secondary seating options have the advantage of being steps, flower pots pedestals and so on every day of the year but can be used as seating when necessary.

In the past it was common for buildings and urban furniture to be designed to be beautiful elements in the pedestrian landscape as well as providing sitting opportunities. Venice has few benches but a wealth of

Left: the location and design of seating is important to the quality of the invitations to stay. The steel tubes present a more problematic solution (Japan).
Right: this good bench in the shaft of sunlight along the house gable invites people to stay (Spain).

urban elements suitable for sitting. "The entire City is sittable" reports William H. Whyte, apropos of Venice, in the film *The Social Life of Small Urban Spaces*.[11]

who sits where?

Generally speaking, children and young people can sit anywhere and on anything. Comfort, climate and materials do not play a significant role. These two groups normally dominate the city's secondary seating. Adults and seniors want more comfort and are considerably more meticulous about choosing where to sit. Comfortable city furniture, preferably with back and arm rests as well as good sitting comfort on "seating-friendly'"materials, is often decisive for whether these groups want to sit down in urban space and stay a while. If the idea of urban space for everyone is to have any meaning, it is particularly important to offer good seating for older people. Young people can always make do.

straight backs and cold bottoms

It was mentioned earlier that longer stays mean lively cities. The extent and length of stays are often crucial to city life. Creating socially viable cities for everyone necessitates staying options for all ages.

Good city space should offer primary seating in the form of benches and chairs, as well as many secondary seating options: stairs, bases of statues, monuments, etc. (sitable sculpture in Copenhagen, lie-sit furniture in HafenCity, Hamburg and seating landscape in front of the Sydney Opera House).

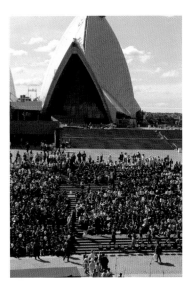

Many designers and architects have a penchant for square stone benches placed decoratively in front of buildings. However, users do not share their affection for this type of uncomfortable city furniture.

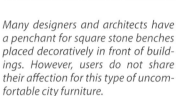

When uncomfortable benches are placed in the middle of city space, it is a good idea to add bronze people to sit on them so they are sure to be occupied (Hasselt, Belgium).

Here is another important area where common architectural practice is on a collision course with the principles for creating city space that is comfortable and attractive for staying. Concern for city life is often totally absent from considerations about the placement of seating and the choice of design and materials for benches. Benches are anchored in the middle of nowhere, far from edges, nooks and crannies, and seating is often designed as plinths or "coffins," which match building blocks in design but not the people who might want to sit on them. Even though marble and polished granite weather beautifully, it is only south of Barcelona that these cold materials are pleasant to sit on, and even then, only for a few months of the year. And without a backrest no one stays very long.

moveable chairs

As mentioned earlier, primary seating can be various types of benches, but can also very well be moveable chairs like the ones in Parisian parks or Bryant Park in New York City. These moveable chairs provide flexibility to users, who can move them around to make the most of the site, climate and view. The freedom to move chairs around provides a valuable opportunity in itself to arrange the social space needed for specific situations.

The simplicity with which moveable chairs can be stored according to season is another advantage. Empty chairs left outside in squares or parks in the cold months stir up memories of a seaside resort in the off-season.

staying in transition zones between private and public space

Up to now discussion has centered on the free pleasures of benches, chairs and inventory details offered to everyone walking through common city space. However, wholly and semiprivate staying options along the edges of common city space also impact on the total activity level. A number of studies of city centers, streets and housing areas show that stays on balconies, terraces and front gardens that skirt city space often make up the bulk of all staying activities.[12] As expected, edge zones to which users have easy access and can furnish and fit out are used more intensively than all the other staying options in the city. The user group is well defined and the option is right at hand.

cappuccino — as a refreshment and an explanation

Of all the staying activities in urban edge zones, sidewalk cafés play a particularly significant role in the modern city landscape. Over the past two or three decades, outdoor service has spread in city space.

While sidewalk cafés were once the province of Mediterranean cities and cultures, the idea has caught on in cities throughout the economically developed part of the world. As city dwellers have become more prosperous and gained more free time, outdoor service has gradually spread from Finland to New Zealand, from Japan to Alaska. Tourists have

Chairs that can be moved around provide comfortable and flexible staying opportunities in the city (City Hall Square, Melbourne, Australia, and Bryant Park, New York City).

cappuccino as a refreshment – and an explanation

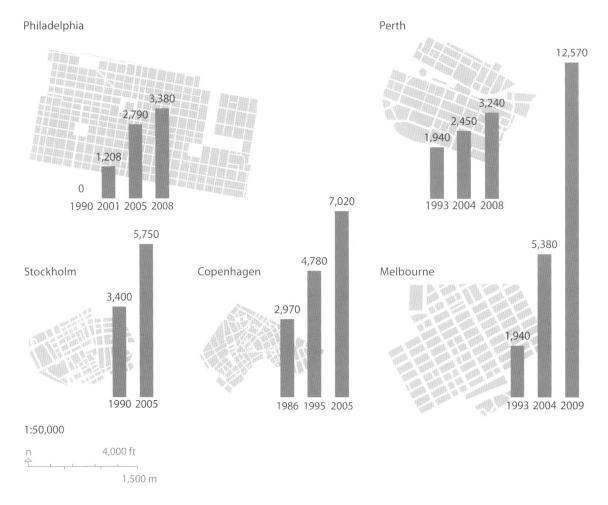

Philadelphia

3,380
2,790
1,208
0

1990 2001 2005 2008

Perth

12,570
3,240
2,450
1,940

1993 2004 2008

Stockholm

5,750
3,400

1990 2005

Copenhagen

7,020
4,780
2,970

1986 1995 2005

Melbourne

5,380
1,940

1993 2004 2009

1:50,000

4,000 ft

1,500 m

Dramatic growth in the number of café chairs found in city space is a worldwide phenomenon. It reflects new needs and new ways of using the city. Coffee cups on tables represent refreshment as well as a good excuse for being in the city – for a long time.[13]

seen recreational city life in outdoor cafés in places they have visited, and brought home the concept of café culture. Whereas cities were once dominated by necessary activities, cafés have brought recreational life into play with a vengeance. Now people have the time and the resources to enjoy the city and city life from the vantage point of café chairs.

As recently as 20 or 30 years ago, many cities, Copenhagen and Melbourne among them, were considered out of the running for outdoor café life due to climate. Each city now has more than 7,000 café chairs in their centers, and cafés have gradually increased the number of months in which they offer outdoor service to eight, ten or twelve, with the 'season' extended year by year.[14]

The popularity of cafés and relatively lengthy stays in them underscores the fact that they offer an attractive combination of options: reasonably comfortable chairs and usually a good view of passersby. The real justification and attraction of sidewalk cafés is precisely that: life on the sidewalk. The opportunity to rest and have refreshments is another plus. Coffee is probably the ostensible reason for someone to be seated at a sidewalk café, but it is also an excuse to watch city life go by. A combination of many attractive options is often the reason for the many café visits. The good reasons also explain why in almost all cases staying times are considerably longer than the time it takes to drink a cup of coffee. The real activity is recreation, time off and pleasure in city space.

In the old days, people spent many hours in city space doing necessary errands and meeting many practical and social needs along the way. Walking and being in the city was an integrated daily activity.

Today there are almost no necessary errands or reasons for spending any appreciable time in city space with the pleasures and delights to follow. In this new situation sidewalk cafés and coffee cups provide new destinations and new reasons for spending hours of time in the city.

a good city is like a good party: guests stay because they are enjoying themselves

In a previous section it was described how life in the city is a product of the number and length of activities, and it has been shown how staying activities and thereby length are the key factor for establishing lively city space and cities. In contrast, many people with short stays in the city do not add much life.

To invite people to walk and bicycle in city space is a beginning, but by no means enough. The invitation must also include the option of sitting down and spending time in the city. Staying activities are the key to a lively city, but also the key to a truly delightful city. People stay in a place if it is a beautiful, meaningful and pleasant place to be. The good city has many similarities to a good party: the guests stay on because they are enjoying themselves.

In recent years café culture has spread rapidly even to regions where the idea would have been unthinkable only a few years ago (summer afternoon, Reykjavik, Iceland).

seeing, hearing and talking — as a common prerequisite

The good city for meeting is essentially a city with good opportunity for three basic human activities: seeing, hearing and talking.

Meeting in city space takes place on many levels. Passive contacts, opportunities to simply see and hear life in the city represents an unpretentious and nonobligating form of contact. To see and be seen is the simplest and by far the most widespread form of meeting between people.

Compared with the number of seeing and hearing contacts, the more active and direct meetings make up a smaller but versatile group. There are planned and spontaneous meetings, unexpected meetings, greetings, verbal exchanges and conversations with acquaintances met on walks. People ask directions and are shown the way. There are conversations with friends and family with whom one is walking through the city. There are conversations on benches, at bus stops and certainly with the person sitting next to you when there is an occasion for it or something unexpected happens. There are events to watch, musicians to listen to and large public events like parades, street parties and demonstrations to look at or participate in.

In various combinations, the opportunities to see, hear and talk are a prerequisite for communication between people in city space.

a good view is essential

Looking at city life is one of the most important and most popular urban attractions. People watching is a universal activity that takes place constantly as we walk, stand or sit. The use of benches and other seating is reinforced if they provide a good view of people. The view of other attractions such as water, trees, flowers, fountains and architecture should also be part of city planners' considerations. The view is even better if several attractions can be combined. Careful thinking about views and options for looking must be part of the effort made for good city quality.

unhindered lines of vision, please

Because a free and unhindered view to city attractions is so vital, the lines of vision must be treated as carefully as the views themselves. In many cities, parked cars and buses, poorly located buildings, inventory and landscaping often limit the view and overview.

Another specific problem is the line of vision from windows and balconies in buildings. Here the view is often blocked by horizontal window bars thoughtlessly positioned just at eye level so that it is not possible for people seated inside to have an unrestricted view. Massive railings on balconies and fences on terraces often block the opportunity to follow life on the street or park from inside the dwellings. For the architect, the secret is to think of what you can see from inside when designing the details, while ensuring that the private lives of the individuals within cannot be unduly invaded from outside.

Here it is also important that the lines of vision for standing, sitting and children's level are studied and naturally incorporated in the sectional drawings of buildings and streets.

visual contact
— to and from buildings

The importance of good visual contact between inside and outside at streets level has been described in a previous section. Visual contact between people in the buildings, particularly on the ground floors and in the public space in front are important to the experience of intensity and contact opportunities for everyone involved, both inside and out.

Again careful planning is paramount so that consideration for experiences and contacts is weighed against consideration for protecting the private sphere. Shops and offices are often able to operate with a great amount of visual accessibility. The transparent Apple stores in major cities demonstrate how life in the shop becomes a visual part of city life. In contrast, many other shopping units, particularly supermarkets, stand in isolation from city life, hermetically sealed with walls of brick, tinted glass or advertising posters, thus doing their part to make city life poorer in experience. Another unfortunate development is the use of massive shutters in front of shop windows outside opening hours. They make streets feel more unsafe and far less interesting to walk down in the evening and on weekends, because there is nothing to look at or experience along these closed façades.

Visual contact between outside and inside adds to the opportunities for experience — in both directions.

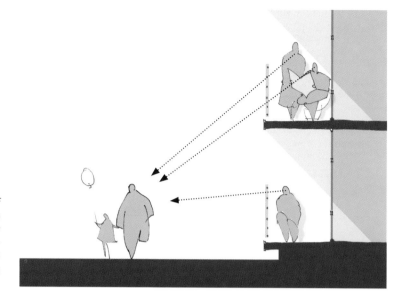

It is important to consider the lines of vision between inside and outside so that people can see out whether they are standing or seated. A wide spectrum of visual experience must be ensured without compromising the private domain.

The balcony railings in Ralph Erskine's residential complexes are typically designed to provide a good downward view (Ekerø, Stockholm, Sweden).

Careful work with lines of vision ensures good visual contact between outside and inside in this residential complex (Sibelius Park, Copenhagen; also see page 102).

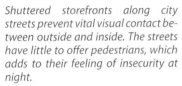

Shuttered storefronts along city streets prevent vital visual contact between outside and inside. The streets have little to offer pedestrians, which adds to their feeling of insecurity at night.

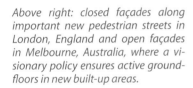

Above right: closed façades along important new pedestrian streets in London, England and open façades in Melbourne, Australia, where a visionary policy ensures active ground-floors in new built-up areas.

The answer to these highly problematic closings is often a city policy to ensure active, visually inviting ground floors. Melbourne is a good example with its requirement that 60% of street façades in new buildings along major streets must be open and inviting. Many cities have implemented similar active ground-floor policies with good results.

In conjunction with housing, many types of partial screening are used to make visual contact possible while ensuring that other people cannot look in. Protection can have the form of screens or landscaping, or it can mean that passersby are kept at a suitable arms-length distance by strategically placed stairs, front gardens and flowerbeds. Or the problem can be elegantly solved using height differences, so that the private dwelling is raised a few steps above street level. This provides a fine view of city life while making sure no one can see in.

hearing and talking

Being able to hear and talk are important qualities in urban public space, however these qualities have gradually been pushed into the background as the noise level of car traffic has grown in cities. The opportunity to meet and carry on a conversation in city space, once taken for granted, has become more and more difficult.

One of the major quality problems in modern city streets is a fluctuating and high noise level that thwarts ordinary conversation.

In pedestrian cities like Venice the noise level is typically under 60 dB. Here it is easy to carry on conversations even over great distances.

A walk in pedestrian-friendly Venice and the traffic-filled streets of London, Tokyo or Bangkok illustrates the dramatic changes that have happened with the sound level in city streets. These walking tours also illustrate the qualities that have been lost in this process.

The quiet is striking from the moment you walk out onto the staircase in front of the railway station in Venice. Suddenly it is possible to hear voices, footsteps, birds and music. Everywhere in Venice it is possible to speak quietly and pleasantly with others. At the same time you can hear footsteps, laughter, snatches of conversation, singing from open windows and many other sounds of life in the city. Both the possibility to hold a conversation and the sound of human activity are important qualities.

Walking in traffic-filled city streets is a completely different experience. The noise from cars, motorcycles and most particularly buses and trucks ricochets between building façades, creating a continuously high noise level that makes it almost impossible to talk to others. Words are shouted with difficulty from person to person, it is necessary for one speaker to shout into the ear of the other, conversational distance must be reduced to the absolute minimum and often assisted by lip reading. Not only has any type of meaningful communication between people been rendered pointless, but the extreme noise level is also a permanent stress factor.

Gradually the people who use these streets grow so accustomed to the noise that they no longer speculate about how the situation has developed. By sticking a finger in the other ear, a person can just manage to carry on a loud conversation in a cell phone.

In these noise dominated cities parks, car-free streets and squares are the spaces where it is still possible to be heard. Suddenly it is once again possible to hear the sound of people and human activity. Street musicians and artists are packed in rather tightly along walking streets: their activities would be meaningless in any other part of the city.

Among the most significant arguments for reducing car traffic in city streets, or at least reducing traffic speed, is that it reduces the noise level and communication between people once again becomes possible.

communication and noise level

A background noise level of 60 decibels (dB) is given as the upper limit, if people are to carry on a normal, varied conversation at an ordinary conversational distance.

Every increase of eight dB leads to the feeling that the noise level has doubled. In other words, the human ear hears 68 dB as twice as loud as 60 dB, and 76 dB is felt as four times the noise level of 60 dB.[15]

The School of Architecture at The Royal Danish Academy of Fine Arts conducted a study in Burano, a small pedestrian enclave in the Venetian Lagoon, and in a traffic street in Copenhagen that shows a connection between communication and noise level in the pedestrian town and the traffic street.[16] In Burano the average noise level in the small local street and the town's main street were measured at 52 dB and 63 dB respectively. So the background noise in the main street is approximately twice as loud as in the local street. In both streets the noise level was rather constant.

Both in the space with 52 dB and that with 63 dB it is possible to carry on a pleasant conversation and often at quite a distance. Conversations are relatively undisturbed across the space of the town's canals or between people on the street and those upstairs in buildings.

In the Copenhagen traffic street the background noise was 72 dB at ordinary traffic intensity, while the noise level varied widely and could reach up to 84 dB when buses and large trucks passed. The 72 dB represents a noise level that is between three and four times greater than background noise in walking streets. Very few conversations take place on this street, and they are typically conducted as the exchange of only a few words and largely only in periods where no noisy vehicles drive down the street.

City furniture can make conversations difficult or even impossible.
Conversely, it can be designed and
set up to offer a wealth of conversational opportunities — as wanted
and needed.

Levels of 60 – 65 dB can be found in many car-free city spaces with some human activity, and represent the sum of the noise from many footsteps, conversations, children at play, resonance from building façades and so on.

In connection with city life studies conducted in London in 2004, in Sydney in 2007, and New York in 2008, background noise of the magnitude of 72 – 75 dB was measured in city center streets.[17]

Difficulties trying to carry out a conversation were noted in all three cities. Particularly in London, the combination of relatively narrow streets, tall buildings and unusually noisy diesel engines in city buses produces a sound climate that precludes ordinary forms of conversation in large sections of the city.

talkscapes

City furniture can make a valuable contribution to meetings in urban space. Long even benches where people sit shoulder to shoulder are appropriate for maintaining the form of keeping an "arm's-length distance" to other people.

While city benches are good for preserving private space and distance, they are not very good for communication. It is possible to turn your head and get a conversation going, but if a group is seated, a family with children or several friends who would like to chat, a row of city benches is not particularly inviting. A far better solution is the grouping of benches into a "talkscape."

Architect Ralph Erskine (1914–2005) worked systematically with talkscapes in all his projects by setting two benches at an angle with a small table facing them so people could talk as well as use the table. The benches were set up at a slightly open angel so that people could choose to be together or alone, which allows for the option of conversation.

It is possible to find great talkscapes in city space where moveable chairs for years have been one of the biggest attractions. From Parisian parks, the idea has spread to many urban spaces, old and new.

Not surprisingly, flat plinths without backrests or any other type of mitigating circumstances are at the bottom of the list of conversational options.

It can be frustrating indeed for a family to try to achieve any type of togetherness on this type of seating crate, which to make matters even worse are almost always situated in the middle of the space far from any screening façades.

The architect must have thought the crates suited the architecture, but they most certainly do not promote any type of urban meeting.

musical meetings

The city is also a meeting place for the exchange of music, performance, sharing talent with others, from a little boy with a recorder to the Salvation Army Band or the Queen's Guards parading and playing at full vol-

City space has served as the meeting place for people for thousands of years, and this function is still one of the most important and most appreciated.

ume through the town. All of these activities are colorful and important types of meetings in city space.

In this area I have a confession and some personal experiences I would like to share. For 30 years I have played trombone in a jazz band at street parties, carnivals, metro station inaugurations and gospel concerts. It is fascinating to play in various city space venues and discover just how dependent music is on space and place. A large expanse of park lawn absorbs most of the sound while the wind blows the rest in all directions, with a disappointing result to follow. In contrast, on squares or in narrow streets in the old city, the music suddenly takes wing — particularly if the space is dimensioned in keeping with human senses. The results here can be that a genuine musical event takes place!

democratic meetings on all levels

The city as meeting place is also a question of the opportunity for democratic exchanges where people have open access to express their happiness, sorrow, enthusiasm or anger at street parties, demonstrations, parades or meetings. Together with the many daily face-to-face meetings with fellow citizens, these common manifestations are an important prerequisite for democracy.

Silent protest marches through the streets of Leipzig, Germany, in 1989 were an important beginning to the end of the Cold War. Student marches every Monday through the streets of Belgrade in 1996 and 1997 were an important precondition for the reinstatement of democracy in Serbia. The silent protest of mothers against the military dictatorship in Argentina every Thursday from 1977 – 2007 on May Square in Buenos Aires is also an example of how brave and meaningful meetings in public space have shaped a better future for people.

World history is full of similar examples that underscore the importance of city space as a meeting place on many levels from quiet conversation to powerful demonstration.

4.5
Self-expression, play, and exercise

new times — new activities

The invitation to people to express themselves, play and exercise in city space covers an important topic with the goal of creating lively, healthy cities. This topic of healthy cities is fairly new and reflects changes in society.

the city as playground

Children's play has always been an integral part of city life. In the past children played where the grown-ups worked and conducted their activities.

The city of Venice has essentially no playgrounds: the city is a playground in itself. Children crawl on monuments and stairs, play along the canals, and if they don't have a playmate nearby they can always kick a soccer ball to one of the passing pedestrians. If a child kicks a ball into the middle of a stream of pedestrians, there is always at least one who will attempt some fast footwork and a return of the ball, a game that can go on for hours.

Modernism's planning requires dedicated playgrounds: "Please play here." The concept of special places for children's play catches on as most Western societies subject themselves to specialization and institutionalization, with schools and after-school programs, and busy, hard-working parents.

more energy and creativity

At the same time that parents get busier at work, they also have more free time, and seen in a larger life perspective, a great deal more free time in fact. That generates the need and energy for many recreational and creative activities, which can often take place in common city space. A great deal of creativity has been unleashed in our society: people play music, sing, dance, play, exercise and engage in sport as never before in public space.

The number of festivals, street parties, cultural evenings, car-free days, parades, waterfront parties and sports events are steadily increasing and attract many people. There is energy and time for people to express themselves.

in good shape — for many years

The number of senior citizens is rising sharply. They represent a new group with needs for walkable infrastructure. They need to be physically active, take long walks, try Nordic walking, bicycle more, etc. The idea is to stay in shape for a lifetime.

have: indoor life
— wanted: fresh air and exercise

For most people working life has changed in terms of the work itself, the workplace and transport. Much work today is primarily stationary, offices are often artificially ventilated, and transit options usually involve sitting in a car or train.

This is a dramatic historical shift from the days when work was physically demanding and conducted outside or in front of open windows, and transport was by foot or bicycle.

No matter how successful we are at improving cities so that they once again invite people to walk and bicycle more, we will still need purpose-built tracks and other facilities where people can meet their need for fresh air and exercise.

new exciting play facilities
and/or good everyday cities

In the face of these new challenges, there is a strong tendency to focus on what is new and special. Play equipment and facilities and many different kinds of sports halls, walking paths, skating lanes and ambitious theme parks with physical challenges are being established for children and sports enthusiasts. Just as with pedestrians and bicyclists we need

Good cities have built-in opportunities for play and self-expression. Simple solutions are often the most convincing.

Fixed
Space, furniture and set up can provide a well-functioning framework for daily life in the city. Inviting fixed frameworks are a crucial prerequisite (Piazza del Campo, Siena, Italy).

Flexible
Initiatives and space for the city's special, often seasonal, activities are needed in addition to daily frameworks and activities (ice sculpture festival in Nuuk, Greenland).

Fleeting
City space must make room for short-term but important activities such as street music, morning gymnastics, parades, festivals and fireworks (Beijing, China).

to provide careful invitations so that the facilities will be used. They promote healthy living and add valuably to life in cities.

However, let us disregard the more spectacular and inspiring new facilities for a moment and focus on the main target of this book: ensuring better conditions for walking and bicycling in cities around the clock every day of the year.

Making such an effort to provide better pedestrian and bicycle cities will obviously also mean better conditions for children, improved opportunities for senior citizens and a stronger invitation to exercise in connection with ordinary daily activities around town. The opportunity for creative and cultural activities is also reinforced when the "everyday city" is improved for human activity and staying.

For the same reason, a good city policy should focus on improvements for the ordinary everyday city space, on integrating into everyday space some challenges and opportunities for children, older people and exercise enthusiasts.

fixed, flexible and fleeting

Precisely the many new challenges to city space, the great creativity and enthusiasm among inhabitants and the many ideas about how to ensure good opportunities for the new needs could tempt planners to establish many spaces for specific age groups and activities. Many good ideas can be built up and secured by instigating extensive public space projects for special purposes. Then the facilities stand ready if anyone has the time or interest in using them.

Instead of a policy emphasizing special space for special activities, a city policy could be based on the principles of the fixed, flexible and fleeting.

The fixed element is the city space, the fixed daily framework on city life. The flexible element is the special temporary facilities and events that may take place in city space during the year: swimming and kayaking in the harbor in the summer, skating rinks in the winter, Christmas market, annual carnival, circus in town, festival week and all the other events that can be established in turns in city space. And finally the fleeting element is the large number of minor events in the city: waterfront festivals, fireworks, concerts on the square, entertainment in parks, midsummer bonfires and so on. At the far end of the scale of fleeting-but-festive events are street musicians, street theater, street parties, poetry reading evenings, to name a few.

The ground structure must be in place (fixed) for a successful city policy for creating cities for people. That the city should have a well-proportioned and inviting city space that inspires all types of activities – flexible and fleeting.

On all the other days it is just a great city.

4.6
Good places, fine scale

good places and fine scale, please

No matter how much work is devoted to climate, lighting, furniture and the many other factors important to city quality at eye level, the effort is almost in vain unless spatial quality, proportions and dimensions are subject to careful scrutiny. The experience of comfort and well being in cities is closely tied to how city structure and city space harmonize with the human body, human senses and corresponding space dimensions and scale. Unless good places and a good human scale are provided, crucial city qualities will be lacking.

where events want to take place

The importance of good places is mentioned often in the previous section. Events, exchanges and conversations take place when there are comfortable, inviting places to stand and sit. The jazz band that discovered some excellent and some terrible places to play tells a story about quality and the specific spatial and acoustic qualities that are sometimes present and other times absent.

From city to city space and all the way down to tiny nooks and crannies, spatial relationships and size have a decisive influence on our experience of place and our desire to move about and stay in just that spot.

quality of scale and place on city level

If we visit traditional cities like Hydra in Greece or Portofino in Italy, we find that the entire city fits the human body and senses. With their mod-

When a whole town fits the human scale and senses (harbor promenade on the island of Hydra in Greece).

*Good places and fine scale
(Ginzan Onsen; Yamagata in Japan).*

quality of scale and place
in city space

est size and semicircular design around the bay, these cities are dimensioned by our senses. We can see the entire entity across the harbour, the city space, all activities, and many details close up. The experience is natural and unforced.

It is possible to get a strong sense of harmony in city space physically and through the senses. Approaching the Piazza del Campo in Siena or the Piazza Navona in Rome one has a sense of "here is the place; I have arrived." In 1889 in his famous review of the spatial qualities of older Italian cities, Camilo Sitte described the importance of dimensioning city space to fit the people and functions they will serve, as well as having closed space where the line of vision is halted by surrounding façades.[18] The size of the spaces is a crucial factor for well-being and for the function of the space as a framework for human activities.

A study of spatial proportions in old cities reveals the same model in city after city. Street widths of 3, 5, 8 or 10 meters/10, 16, 26 or 33 feet can easily handle pedestrian streams of between 2,400 and 7,800 people per hour. The squares often approach the magical 40 x 80 meters/131 x 262 feet in size, which means that people can take in the entire scene, seeing the square itself and the faces of other people when they walk through the space. Corresponding proportions are often found in holiday resorts, amusement parks and shopping centres, where visitors' comfort as well as the desire to make every meter/foot count determines the dimensions of space.

too big, too cold and too dismissive — in many new cities

The situation is quite different in many new city areas, which typically end up with space that is too large and amorphous. Large buildings and many moving and parked cars may explain why overly large spaces have been established, but as a framework for pedestrian activity and stays they are a poor excuse. Not many human activities can "take place" here. Everything is too large, too cold and too dismissive.

on dealing with the slow and rapid scales separately

The very different requirements of 5 km/h (3 mph) architecture and 60 km/h (35 mph) architecture must logically lead to treating the different types of space separately, or even better, collecting the activities in space that is carefully articulated, so that the small scale is used along façades and the rapid scale along lanes of motorized traffic. In this connection, pedestrian prioritized streets provide a special opportunity to work with 5 km/3 mph architecture, so that pedestrians can move about in comfort and slow-moving vehicles can be allowed access.

on treating the human landscape and large buildings separately

Successful interplay between the small scale and the slightly larger. Boat houses in front of residential area (Slusehol-men, Copenhagen, Denmark).

The problem of overly large modern buildings placed more or less at random in the city landscape, landing with a bang on sidewalks with no transitions or mitigating circumstances, has already been mentioned. Regarding quality of place and modest dimensions, the principle should be to build cities that are attractive and cohesive at eye level and put larger buildings on top.

The principle of small spaces in larger ones can often ensure well-functioning small spaces in the larger space of the city (arcades, tree-lined boulevards and market stalls in Guatemala, Spain and Singapore).

small spaces in larger ones

The principle of putting small spaces into a larger space is another method of combining large space and modest human scale. Many old cities and city spaces use colonnades and archways. Pedestrians can move about in an intimate and delimited space in a colonnade, while having a view and overview of the larger city space. Small spaces can also be established in a larger space using allés or rows of trees. A good example is the Rambla in Barcelona, where the main pedestrian space is separated from the larger city space by kiosks and two rows of shady trees. Another example is market stalls on a square or the umbrellas and awnings at sidewalk cafés that make city spaces seem smaller and more intimate. Furniture and bollards can also help create small spaces in large, such as the row of bollards in the Piazza del Campo in Siena.

when the small scale must be dropped by parachute — after the fact

Using small bushes and umbrellas, this café is trying to create a useful small scale in a much too large city space (St. Pölten, Austria).

Middle left and right: when all dimensions are too large, it is difficult and often impossible to get the important small scale to function afterwards (Eurolille, Lille, France).

In Ørestad, Copenhagen, Denmark, chairs that can be moved around try to make up for the lack of small scale.

when the small scale must be
dropped by parachute
— after the fact

Unfortunately, new cities are still being built according to principles that shatter the scale. There are too many spaces, they are too large, and the human landscape is therefore cold and dismissive or even completely unusable.

Once the damage is done, it is usually extremely difficult to take effective steps to remedy the situation. Buildings have been erected, entrance doors are sited, city furniture and equipment delivered, and the money all spent before anyone thinks that some utterly essential qualities are missing: place quality and the human scale. In this situation, the small scale must be brought into the large space literally by parachute, using pergolas, kiosks, landscaping, groups of trees, awnings, plants and furniture to reduce the dimensions of the space. Efforts must be made to establish small intimate and approachable space where people will want to be. It is expensive and difficult, and the results far from as good as they might have been if place quality and human scale had been part of the building program from the start.

as long as the cats are happy...

Even though much can have gone wrong in the larger scheme of things, it is possible now and again to establish good places on the small scale. Sometimes simple elements can make a decisive difference. A bench in the corner under a tree. A place.

One of my students reminded me how much we can learn from cats about good places. When a cat comes out on the doorstep, it stops and slowly checks out the surroundings, after which it carefully moves towards the indisputably best "place" in order to curl up with majestic dignity.

The moral of this story is that "when you build cities you must always keep in mind making the cats happy — then you can be sure that people will be happy too."

*Small spaces and large vehicles
(Hydra, Greece).*

macro-, local and microclimate

Few topics have greater significance for comfort and well-being in city space than the actual climate right where one is sitting, walking or biking. Work with climate and climate protection concentrates on three levels of climate: macro-, local and micro-. Macroclimate is general regional climate. Local climate is the climate in cities and built environments, moderated by the topography, landscape and buildings. Microclimate is the climate in a local atmospheric zone. It can be as small as a single street, in nooks and crannies and around a bench in city space.

good weather — one of the most important criterias

Good weather is one of the most significant criteria for assuring the ease of people's movement in cities, or at least weather as good as it gets given the situation, place and season.

Weather is a favorite topic of conversation everywhere. Postcards the world over feature pictures of relentless rain or thick fog with captions like "spring, summer, autumn and winter" in Dublin, Bergen, Auckland or Seattle. The postcards often concentrate on bad weather days and the general preoccupation with them. But in most regions, most days of the year are in fact quite acceptable. There is a misleading tendency to forget the great majority of days that are not bad. No one is in any doubt about when the weather is good, however, and it brings forth universal smiles.

The opportunity to enjoy good weather is an important city quality (Summer day, Reykjavik, Iceland).

Climate and comfort vary with the seasons and geographic location. Sun is a big attraction in temperate regions, while shade is a prized quality in warmer climates (above left at Tiananmen Square in Beijing, China, seeking shade in Australia and a spring day in Denmark).

In Scandinavia, when the sun shines and the wind is a whisper, the collective mood rises and people greet each other with comments about the lovely weather. It doesn't seem to matter whether the temperature is –10C/14F or +25 C/77 F. When the sun is shining and the wind is tame, it is a good day at Nordic latitudes.

Underlying the satisfaction is the fact that an influx of solar heat and absence of cooling wind means that the microclimate can quickly be brought up to the comfort zone that invites people to stay outdoors even on cold days. Skiers can take long breaks on the sunny side of ski huts or a hillock, sheltered from the wind. The air is cold but the temperature we feel on our skin is pleasant.

the comfort zone

Several climate factors influence the feeling of comfort: air temperature, humidity, wind chill and solar heat. Personal factors such as the way

wind as a serious problem

Tall free-standing buildings always create problems in windy regions where they typically influence wind direction as well as speed (wind conditions behind the Washington Monument in Washington, DC).

Even on relatively calm days, wind conditions near tall buildings can be very unpleasant for pedestrians (street in front of high rise building, Copenhagen, Denmark).

we're dressed and basic physiological differences also play a role. The fat layers and circulatory systems of human bodies vary from region to region, influencing our ability to maintain or radiate heat. These differences mean that comfort zones vary geographically, although differences are minor.

In the following, discussion is rooted in the climatic conditions and climate-related cultural features that characterize northern and central Europe. Corresponding temperate climate conditions are also found in considerable parts of North America, Asia and Australasia.

If the sun is strong, we can usually manage to maintain comfort without wearing insulating clothing. If the sun is weaker, we need a sweater. If the balance between solar heat and cold wind results in an even colder microclimate, we can still be comfortable if we walk, run or bicycle. In Scandinavia, the spring months bring hordes of children outside to play active spring games after a long dark winter. The children hop, jump rope, play ball, roller skate or skateboard. They can sit in comfort in sunny corners, but out in the open they have to keep moving to stay warm.

wind is a serious problem near tall buildings

It is characteristic for macro-, local and microclimates to be very different in given situations. Local climate in city space and parks can be almost pleasant if there is shelter from the wind and some sun, even when strong cold winds are sweeping over the open landscape.

In temperate climate zones where it is important for people to stay warm and avoid chilling, protection against cooling by the wind plays a key role in the climate between buildings.

The wind has free rein in open landscapes, but wind speed is reduced somewhat by friction with the terrain and landscaping. Wind speed along the terrain is further reduced if there are many trees and clustered low buildings. This combination often provides such strong friction that fast, cold winds are diverted above the buildings so that there is almost no wind at all between them.

Friction along the terrain is key in minimizing the effect of the wind. A smooth terrain surface gives the wind free play. In contrast, the wind is slowed dramatically and cooling reduced significantly if the terrain surface is "bumpy," as is the case with woods or cities with many trees and low buildings.

Tall freestanding buildings have the exact opposite effect. Tall buildings capture the fast-moving winds at 30 – 40 meters/90 – 120 feet, while a complicated interplay of high and low pressure can cause wind speed at the foot of tall buildings to be up to four times greater than in the surrounding open landscape. This makes the climate around tall buildings considerably colder, drastically reducing the growth conditions for plants — and people![19]

building with the weather

At the building scale, design has traditionally been carefully adapted to local climate conditions, in order to reduce undesirable influences and exploit the desirable aspects of the climate.

In countries with strong sun and high temperatures, city structure features shady narrow streets and buildings with thick walls and small openings.

Colder climates call for a different strategy. In Scandinavia where the angle of sunlight is low, frequent winds bring warm air overland from the Atlantic Ocean, one of the reasons it has been possible to live and grow crops in this region.

The old cities in the region have carefully adapted to the low angle of sunlight and almost constant wind. Buildings, typically between two and three stories high with slanted roofs, are clustered. Streets, squares and gardens are small and the many trees between buildings provide shade and shelter.

The low-density buildings in old Scandinavian towns are convincingly functional in the local climate. Cold winds are diverted over the rooftops while the sun warms up walls and street surfaces. These conditions make it feel as if the climate has moved many hundreds of kilometers/ miles south (Gudhjem, Denmark).

Tall, free-standing buildings intensify the wind and create turbulence along the ground. It is cold and windy between buildings, and fences are needed to keep the sand from blowing out of sandboxes. The climate at eye level seems to have been shifted many hundreds of kilometers/miles north (residential area with tall buildings, Landskrona, Sweden).

This pattern means that the wind is carried up above the cities, leaving streets and gardens almost free from wind. The low buildings and slanted roofs allow the sun's rays to penetrate between buildings, warming the masonry and cobbled pavements so that the microclimate in the small city spaces is considerably better than the climate in surrounding landscapes.

In these cities it is as if the local climate has moved 1,000 km (600 miles) south, and vegetation therefore includes fig trees, grapevines and palm trees, which do not otherwise thrive this far north. The annual number of hours that can comfortably be spent outdoors is typically twice as great in these traditional built environments than in the region generally.[20]

As pointed out previously, lengthy outside stays mean lively cities. Optimal conditions for outdoor life have been created in old Scandinavian cities precisely because of the careful consideration given to local climate.

building despite the weather

Considering the key role of climate in determining city quality, pleasure and comfort, it is highly unfortunate that most city planning makes no attempt to ensure the best possible natural climate quality in city space.

In many warm regions, extensive road systems, asphalt parking lots and hard roofing materials raise the air temperature from high to unacceptable, whereas trees, lawns, green roofs and porous paving stone would have lowered it. In contrast, high-rise after high-rise is being built in cool, windy regions, increasing wind speed and cooling around the buildings and making outside stays virtually impossible.

umbrellas in Venice, Amsterdam and Rotterdam

Wind from the sea is a constant feature in the many European countries along the coast of the Atlantic Ocean and North Sea, that is, Ireland, England, Scotland, Iceland, Western Norway and Denmark, as well as the French and Dutch coasts along the English Channel. The wind is not as omnipresent in other European regions.

In Venice pedestrians use umbrellas as protection from rain, which usually falls vertically. In Rotterdam, rebuilt after World War II, the city center is dominated by high-rises and local climate reacts accordingly. Here the rain is often horizontal due to the fierce winds that sweep through the streets from all directions due to the tall buildings. On windy rainy days pedestrians wielding umbrellas have their work cut out for them. In Rotterdam people protect their umbrellas, rather than the other way round. The climate is far better in Amsterdam due to an entirely more appropriate city structure. Even though the wind blows freely, it often glides above the city center, which improves the framework for city life considerably.

Naturally, building all over the world should be adapted to local conditions in order to avoid having a negative impact on city environments.

more wind and less sun: no thanks! Example San Francisco

San Francisco's location on the coast of the Pacific Ocean means that the city has lower air temperatures and more wind than just a short distance inland. For the same reason outdoor activities in city space are dependent on sunshine and shelter for a good part of the year. When there are ample amounts of both, San Francisco is a wonderful city for walking and staying.

In the beginning of the 1980s, a plan for the city center opened the possibility for extensive building of new high-rises. Many of the proposed skyscrapers would have created considerably more shadow and stronger winds in major streets and squares, in Chinatown for one.

Students and researchers at the University of California, Berkeley, under the guidance of Professor Peter Bosselmann, conducted a series of studies showing the dependence of San Francisco's city life on sun and shelter. A number of model experiments documented that the new city plan would cast shadows and increase wind in many of the city's key areas. The problems were also illustrated in a documentary film that borrowed Mark Twain's famous quote for its title: "The coldest winter I ever spent was a summer in San Francisco."[21] Local discussion on city quality, climate and new skyscrapers resulted in a referendum that simply asked voters if they wanted less sun and more wind in the city. Needless to say there was no majority support for that policy, and a new city plan adopted in 1985 set out requirements that new built environments near key city spaces must not impoverish the climate. New buildings would have to be kept low or built like steps so that the sun could reach the streets, and wind-tunnel experiments had to document that the buildings would not create wind problems.

In practice these new regulations have meant that no skyscrapers have been built in the regulated areas of downtown San Francisco since 1985. The case of San Francisco provides documentation that it is possible to have high-density building and still ensure a good climate around new buildings.[22]

careful climate planning in new towns

Principles and experiences from San Francisco can be used to advantage in planning new built environments in existing as well as new city areas. Studies must be made from region to region to determine the climate factors that influence comfort and outdoor stays in cities. New buildings must be required to contribute to improved climate conditions in nearby city space.

If cities are to invite people to walk and bicycle more as well as to develop lively and attractive city areas, then climate between buildings is one of the most important target areas. Careful climate planning should be a requirement for all new building.

careful climate planning on the smallest scale

Regardless of the amount of focus on climate planning in city and development plans, it is always possible to improve microclimate — particularly around the places that want to invite people to stay, where microclimate requirements are particularly stringent.

Landscaping, hedges and fences can provide shelter exactly where most needed. There is a lot of innovation and creativity shown around the world, especially in the interests of extending the season for outdoor cafés. There are good economic arguments for ensuring that café chairs can be used as many hours per day and per year as possible.

Oslo, the Norwegian capital in the far north, is a good place to study the innovation and considerations that make it possible for café chairs to be in use outdoors largely all year.

Café areas are framed by glass walls and covered with awnings, heat is provided by heat lamps, electrical fittings or heated floors, and café chairs are selected carefully so that they are warm to sit in. Pillows in chair seats and blankets provided for the backs and legs of guests complete the local microclimate. One can stay at these cafés for a long time almost despite wind and weather.

careful climate planning
on all levels

As the most natural thing in the world, both macro- and local climate should be subject to much more careful work in hot, temperate and cold regions. Large benefits could be reaped at all planning levels and therefore also for the microclimate that creates the necessary good conditions for the human dimension.

If the invitation to walk and bicycle in cities is to be genuine, and if people really want to be inspired and invited to take their time in the city, then microclimate at eye level must be as optimal as possible. There is a lot that can be done. This does not require large investments but rather precise requirements and a great deal of consideration.

In the 1960s no one would have believed that there would ever be outdoor café service in the Scandinavian countries. Today café chairs are in use for 10 – 12 months of the year. New needs and increased awareness of climate conditions have measurably raised comfort and extended the outdoor season (November scene with pillows and blankets, Copenhagen).

Windscreens, awnings, heat lamps and pillows in chairs help provide an acceptable micro-climate in winter months (sidewalk café in Oslo, Norway).

concern for visual quality must
include all urban elements

At eye level the good city provides opportunities for walking, staying, meeting and expression, and that means it must provide good scale and good climate. Common to these desired objectives and quality requirements is that they deal largely with physical and practical matters.

In contrast, work with the city's visual quality is more general. It deals largely with the design and detail of individual elements, and how all the elements are coordinated. Visual quality involves total visual expression, aesthetics, design and architecture.

City space can be designed so that all practical requirements are met, but randomly combined details, materials and colors rob it of visual coordination.

In contrast, city space can be designed with dominating emphasis on aesthetics to the neglect of functional aspects. That the space is beautiful and the details carefully designed is a quality in itself, but far from enough if basic requirements for security, climate, and opportunities for staying are not met.

Results are convincing when design and content are unified (Pioneer Courthouse Square, Portland, Oregon).

The important aspects of city space must be interwoven into a convincing whole.

The interplay between functional and spatial qualities has been convincingly treated in Piazza del Campo in Siena, Italy, one of the reasons the square has served as a meeting place for 700 years.

100% places

In his book, *City: Rediscovering the Center* (1988), William H. Whyte introduces the concept of the 100% place.[23] As the name implies, 100% places are the spaces and localities where all important city space qualities are present. Practical concerns for users' needs merge seamlessly with concern for detail and totality: here is where people want to be.

Perhaps the world-famous Piazza del Campo in Siena became famous precisely because this city square offers that rare combination of qualities. All functional and practical needs are convincingly met. It is safe and comfortable to walk, stand, sit, listen and talk here. In addition, all elements have been merged into a convincing architectural whole, where proportions, materials, colors and details reinforce and enrich the other qualities of the space. Piazza del Campo is a well-functioning and very beautiful city space that for 700 years has served and continues convincingly to serve as Siena's main square. Concern for the human dimension is never outdated.

celebrating the delights of place

In addition to independent work with space and details, it is often possible to make significant quality improvements if a city space is designed to highlight special qualities at the site. New and attractive combinations are possible when city space can be linked directly to water surfaces and quay edges, when contact with parks, flowers and landscaping can be ensured, when spaces can be oriented perfectly in terms of local climate.

Topography and height differences also provide good opportunities to add value. Any differences in height can enhance experiences for pedestrians compared to walking on flat surfaces. New views and experiences pop up. The streets of San Francisco are full of this type of possibility, however minor differences in height can also provide drama at eye level.

art in city space: example Melbourne

City space as a gallery for contemporary art was one of the goals of the art policy adopted in Melbourne, Australia. In addition to works on permanent display, installations and temporary artistic additions to the city landscape are featured, particularly in lanes.

Artistic treatment of light is an important element in the city's overall art policy (Melbourne, Australia).

Views of attractions near and far also enrich city space. Being able to look at a lake, the sea, a landscape or distant mountains is much in demand as a city space quality.

aesthetic quality — for all senses

There is inherent potential in working with visual and aesthetic elements. For people walking through the city, beautiful space, carefully planned details and genuine materials provide valuable experiences on their own merits and as a valuable extra layer to the other qualities the city has to offer.

Naturally, squares and streets can also be designed specifically to provide visual experiences. Here the design and details of the space play a very important role, which can be expanded and reinforced by appealing to the other senses by providing trickling water, fog, steam, aromatic and sound impressions, for example. The main attraction of these spaces is not just city life as such, but rather a potpourri of sensory impressions.

Throughout history, art has made a valuable quality contribution to city space through monuments, sculptures, fountains, building details and decorations. Art communicates beauty, monumentality, remembrance of important events, comments on life in society, fellow inhabitants and city life, together with surprises and humor. Now as ever, city space can serve an important function as an interface between art and people.

In recent years in central parts of Melbourne, efforts to combine art policy and city space policy have served as an inspiring example. The goal has been for the city's common space to serve as a versatile gallery for contemporary art, so that when the people of Melbourne are in the city, they will meet carefully selected and well-placed works of contemporary artists from many disciplines. A three-pronged art policy ensures that selections are current and provide a wealth of experience. The three focus areas are works on permanent display, temporary works and installations, and extensive communication about art to the inhabitants of the city through art centers. One particular emphasis is interactive opportunities for children based on the principle: come and learn more about what you see in the city.

The city policy of emphasis on installations and temporary works makes a valuable contribution to the attractive selection of experiences and unpredictability. Along the city's many narrow lanes and arcades, changing artists decorate spaces with intensity, fantasy and humor, but only for a limited number of months. Then other artists are invited to work on other passageways. There is always something new to look at, and many surprising and humorous comments to discover about the site, the city and contemporary life.

beautiful cities — green cities

Trees, landscaping and flowers play a key role among the elements in city space. Trees provide shade in warm summer months, they cool and cleanse the air, define city space and help accentuate important sites. A

Beautiful cities are green cities. Five hundred new trees are planted in central Melbourne, Australia every year (Swanston Street in Melbourne, 1995 and 2010).

large tree on a square signals: "This is the place." Trees along boulevards underscore a linear sequence, and trees that stretch their branches over the street hint of the presence of green space in the city.

In addition to their immediate aesthetic qualities, the green elements in the city have a symbolic value. The presence of green elements passes on a message about recreation, introspection, beauty, sustainability and the diversity of nature.

After many years in which trees were felled to make room for traffic, or simply died due to poor growth conditions and pollution, there has been a welcome renaissance of green elements in cities more recently. Efforts to improve the conditions for city life and bicyclists are often combined with planting new trees and expanding green urban areas. Every year since 1995, 500 new trees have been planted along streets in Melbourne as part of the city's urban renewal policy, and in accordance with a plan adopted in 2008, New York City's goal is to plant one million new trees in public spaces across the city.[24] The many new green elements make a crucial contribution to city quality while reinforcing New York's wanted profile as a sustainable green metropolis.

beautiful cities — also at night

The lighting in city space has a great impact on orientation, security and visual quality in the dark hours.

Many different lighting strategies are used around the world. One extreme is cities in the USA that have abandoned street lighting under the pretext that motor vehicles light up the night. Needless to say, these areas are usually as dark as a tomb and there is not much for people to look forward to after the sun goes down.

A variety of principles are employed in areas that do use lighting. Many cities are pragmatic and functional in their approach. Lighting principles have often changed during various periods of urban construction and expansion, leaving many types of lamps and various colors of light, which typically results in a random and visually chaotic city scene when night falls.

Other cities have taken a very conscious approach to lighting, recognizing the great impact it has on city quality, as well as its potential as an independent artistic means of expression.

In Melbourne city lighting is a natural part of the city's overall art policy program "Light as Art."

Lyon, France is another good example of a city that has adopted a well-considered artistic lighting policy that takes into account both light setting and color.

Valuable innovations in work with the visual appearance of space at night can also be seen at the city space level. One good example is the Town Hall Square in Sankt Pölten, Austria (1995 – 97), which employs indirect reflected light and a light setting that varies according to time of year and the events being held on the square.

Lighting is the focus of conscious artistic treatment in many cities. Pioneering efforts were made in Lyon in the years after 1990 (Rue de la Republique, Lyon, France).

Water, fog, steam, materials, colors, surfaces, light and sound in many combinations can contribute to an attractive diversity of sensory impressions in city space.

last but not least...

The criteria for good city quality in pedestrian landscapes are summarized in a 12-point keyword list on page 239. Point 12 is positive sensory experiences. The reason for listing this point last is that visual quality is an umbrella concept that should include all of the elements in the city landscape. The placement also represents a conscious underscoring of the fact that visual quality cannot ensure city quality on its own, but that good cities at eye level are created by working on all 12 quality criteria together.

If cities are to function and invite people to enjoy them, under all circumstances, the physical, practical and psychological aspects must be thoroughly treated and then enhanced with valuable layers through work on visual qualities.

This connection is emphasized because although many projects do a fine job of developing the visual aspects, they neglect other more pragmatic qualities.

All over the world are examples of city districts and city space where visual and aesthetic considerations have unilaterally dominated design. Perhaps these urban projects and urban spaces will be pictured in architecture magazines, but in the real world these city spaces typically work poorly or not at all, because key consideration for people and life in public space is missing.

All quality criteria must be part of deliberations — every time.

4.9
Good cities for bicycling

bicyclists as part of city life

Bicyclists represent a different and somewhat rapid form of foot traffic, but in terms of sensory experiences, life and movement, they are part of the rest of city life. Naturally, bicyclists are welcome in support of the goal to promote lively, safe, sustainable and healthy cities.

In the following, planning good cities for bicyclists is handled relatively narrowly and in direct relation to discussion on the human dimension in city planning.

although many are suitable — there are very few good bicycle cities

Around the world there are numerous cities where bicycles and bicycle traffic would be unrealistic. It is too cold and icy for bicycles in some areas, too hot in others. In some places the topography is too mountainous and steep for bicycles. Bicycle traffic is simply not a realistic option in those situations. Then there are surprises like San Francisco, where you might think bicycling would be impractical due to all the hills. However, the city has a strong and dedicated bicycle culture. Bicycling is also popular in many of the coldest and warmest cities, because, all things considered, even they have a great number of good bicycling days throughout the year.

The fact remains that a considerable number of cities worldwide have a structure, terrain and climate well suited for bicycle traffic. Over the years, many of these cities have thrown their lot in with traffic policies that prioritized car traffic and made bicycle traffic dangerous or completely impossible. In some places extensive car traffic has kept bicycle traffic from even getting started.

In many cities, bicycle traffic continues to be not much more than political sweet talk, and bicycle infrastructure typically consists of unconnected stretches of paths here and there rather than the object of a genuine, wholehearted and useful approach. The invitation to bicycle is far from convincing. Typically in these cities only one or two percent of daily trips to the city are by bicycle, and bicycle traffic is dominated by young, athletic men on racing bikes. There is a yawning gap from that situation to a dedicated bicycle city like Copenhagen, where 37% of traffic to and from work or school is by bicycle. Here bicycle traffic is more sedate, bicycles are more comfortable, the majority of cyclists are women, and bicycle traffic includes all age groups from school children to senior citizens.

Bicyclists on their way through the city are part of city life. Furthermore they can with ease switch between being bicyclists and pedestrians.

At a time when fossil fuel, pollution and problems with climate and health are increasingly becoming a global challenge, giving higher priority to bicycle traffic would seem like an obvious step to take. We need good cities to bike in and there are a great many cities where it would be simple and cheap to upgrade bicycle traffic.

a whole-hearted bicycle policy

The cities that have successfully promoted bicycle traffic in recent decades can be tapped for good ideas and requirements for becoming a good bicycle city. Copenhagen is a compelling example of a city whose longstanding bicycle tradition came under threat from car traffic in the 1950s and 1960s. However, the oil crises in the 1970s were the catalyst for a targeted approach to inviting people to ride their bicycles more. And the message was received: today bicycles make up a considerable part of city traffic, and have helped keep vehicular traffic at an unusually low level compared to other large cities in Western Europe. The experiences from Copenhagen are used in the following to provide a platform for discussion about the good bicycle city.

a bicycle network from door to door

In Copenhagen, a cohesive network for bicycles comprising all parts of the city has gradually been established. Traffic is so quiet on small side streets and residential streets in 15 and 30 km per hour/9 and 19 mph zones that a special cycle network is not necessary, but all major streets have one. On most streets, the network consists of bicycle paths along the sidewalks, typically using the curbstones as dividers toward the sidewalk, as well as parking and driving lanes. In some places bike lanes are not delimited by curbstones, but rather marked with painted stripes inside a row of parked cars, so that the cars protect the bicycles from motorized traffic. In fact, this system is known as "Copenhagen-style bicycle lanes."

bicycles in an integrated transport policy: example Copenhagen

Bicycle traffic should be automatically integrated into an overall transport strategy. If it is possible to take bicycles on the train, subway and by taxi, then travel can be combined over great distances (examples from Copenhagen, Denmark).

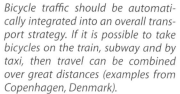

Another link in the city's bicycle system is green bicycle routes, which are dedicated bike routes through city parks and along discontinued railway tracks. These paths are intended for bicycles in transit and are viewed as a supplementary opportunity, a sightseeing possibility and a green option for bicycles. However, the main principle of bicycle policy is for bicycles to have room on ordinary streets, where just like the others in traffic, their owners have errands in shops, residences and offices. The principle is for bicycle traffic to be safe from door to door throughout the city.

Room for this comprehensive bicycle network has been largely gained by down-sizing car traffic. Parking space and driving lanes have been gradually reduced, as traffic patterns have moved from car to bicycle traffic, and therefore bicycles needed more room. Most of the city's major four-lane streets have been converted to two-lane streets with two bicycle paths, two sidewalks and a broad median strip intended to make it safer for pedestrians to cross the street. Roadside trees have been planted and traffic is two-way as before.

Bicycle paths are placed along sidewalks in the same direction as vehicular traffic, and are always on the right and thus "slow" side of vehicular traffic. That way all traffic groups know — more or less — where they have the bicycles, which is the safest system for all parties.

bicycles as part of integrated transport thinking

The invitation to bike must mean that bicycle traffic is integrated into the overall transport strategy. It has to be possible to bring bikes on trains and the metro lines, and preferably in city buses so that it is possible to travel by combining bike trips with public transport. Taxis too must be able to transport bicycles when needed.

Another important link in an integrated transport policy is the possibility to park bicycles securely at stations and traffic hubs. Good bicycle parking options are also needed along streets in general, at schools, offices and dwellings. New offices and industrial buildings should include bicycle parking, changing rooms and showers for bicyclists as a natural part of their planning.

a safe bicycle network, please

Traffic safety is a crucial element in overall bicycle strategies. A cohesive bicycle network protected by curbstones and parked cars is an important first step. Another key concern is the experienced and real safety of the city's intersections. Copenhagen is working on several strategies. Large intersections have special bicycle lanes of blue asphalt and bicycle icons to remind drivers to watch out for bicycles. Intersections also have special light signals for bicycles, which typically give a green light to bicycle traffic six seconds before cars are allowed to move. Trucks and buses are required to have special bicycle mirrors and frequent media campaigns admonish drivers to watch out for bicycles, particularly at intersections.

the more bicycles, the safer the bicyclists

The risk of accidents and actual accidents fall drastically when more people bicycle. Car drivers keep a much better eye on bicycle traffic when there are many bicycles on the street. Right: graph showing increase in bicycling and reduction in accidents from 1996 to 2008 (Copenhagen, Denmark).[25]

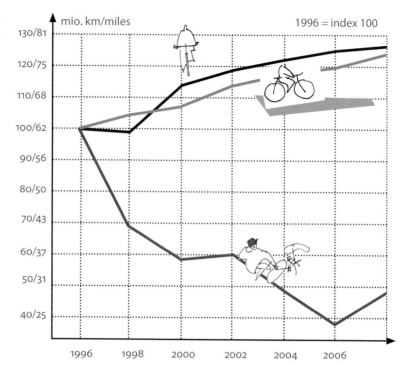

■ Km/miles cycled (mio km/ miles per weekday)

▨ Km/miles of bicycle path, bicycle lane and green routes

▨ Number of bicyclists seriously injured

Good bicycle cities know that good visibility at intersections is vital. In Denmark vehicles are not allowed to park closer than 10 meters/33 feet from an intersection for this very reason.

The widespread American practice of allowing cars to "turn right on red" at intersections is unthinkable in cities that want to invite people to walk and bicycle.

safety in numbers
— also for bicycles

The volume of bicycle traffic is one of the most significant safety factors for making bicycle systems safe. The more bicycles there are, the more it forces drivers to watch out for bicyclists and be constantly on guard. There is a considerable positive effect when bicycle traffic reaches a reasonable "critical mass."

a comfortable network

It is also relevant to mention comfort and amenity value in terms of bicycle networks. Bicycle trips can be pleasant, interesting and free of unnecessary irritations, or they can be boring and difficult. Many of the criteria for good places to walk can be transferred to bicycle routes.

It is important for bicycles to have enough room so that they won't be pushed or crowded. Bicycle paths in Copenhagen vary in width from 1.7 to 4 meters/5.5 to 13 feet, with 2.5 meters/8.2 feet as the recommended minimum.

As bicycle traffic is gradually developed into a versatile, popular transport system, many new and wider bicycles appear on the street scene. These include three-wheeled transport bicycles for children and goods,

Recently, key bicycle lanes in Copenhagen have been widened to overcome the increasing congestion on bicycle lanes (Copenhagen, Denmark).

bicycle cities and city bicycles

handicap bicycles and bicycle taxis. All of these transport options require room, and senior bikers as well as the many parents who transport their children by bicycle need increased reassurance that they won't be pushed and crowded. As bicycle traffic successfully develops as an alternative transport system, more room is needed. Despite the new demands for more room, the bicycle continues to be the superior means of wheeled transport, which requires the smallest amount of room per person in the streets of the city.

A study conducted in Copenhagen in 2005 concluded that one of the city's most pressing problems was heavy congestion on bicycle paths. The city council has since adopted an expansion of the width of bicycle paths in the most popular streets and is underway carrying out this policy.[26]

Frequent interruptions are irritating and destroy the rhythm of the bicycle trip. Over the years Copenhagen has introduced several solutions to reduce the problem. Bicycle paths are often carried across minor side streets without interruption, which results in bicycle trips with fewer interruptions and lets drivers know they must wait. Introducing green waves for bicycles on selected street helps correspondingly to reduce irritating stops. In order to create these green bicycle waves, stoplights are set so that when bicycles bike at about 20 km/h (12.4 mph) they need not stop when they bike to and from the city during rush hour. That service used to be provided for cars. Another form of comfort and safety for bicyclists in Copenhagen is the city practice of snow removal. The bicycle lanes are always cleared before driving lanes to emphasize bicycle priority and the invitation to bike — despite the season.

In recent years, many cities have introduced various types of city bicycles that can be borrowed or rented from stands or depots. The idea is to reinforce bicycle traffic by making it easier for people to use bicycles for short trips in the city, while providing a collective bicycle system so that individuals do not need to buy, store and repair their own bicycles.

Amsterdam's white bicycle bike-share system came and disappeared quickly from the street scene in the 1970s. More stable and well-organized systems were established in the 1990s, in Copenhagen, for example. Today Copenhagen has 2,000 city bicycles available at 110 bicycle stations in the city center. The bicycles are free, financed by advertisements. Users pay a coin deposit, which is returned when the borrowed bicycle is returned to one of the official bicycle racks. Copenhagen's city bikes are used primarily by tourists, who can bicycle around town easily and safely, thanks to the well developed bicycle network. Copenhageners rarely borrow city bicycles, because they prefer their own bikes. In brief, the principle underlying city bikes in Copenhagen is to enable inexperienced city bicyclists to ride around in a relatively safe bicycling environment.

Reasonably wide bicycle paths, the protection of curbstones, bicycle crossings at intersections, special traffic lights that turn green six seconds before cars, and "green waves" that ensure that bicycles can ride through town with no stopping are part of the elements in the very successful bicycle policy in Copenhagen.

When it snows, bicycle paths are cleared before streets for vehicular traffic.

City bike programs have by now been introduced in numerous European cities, among others, in Paris, where the pattern of use is different from that in Copenhagen. Here under the Vélib program, city bicycles are used primarily by Parisians themselves. By renting a Vélib by the hour, week or year, they are able to ride a bike without the trouble of storing and maintaining it. The bicycle rental companies handle the bother in return for the rental fees they charge the bicyclists.

During 2008 the Vélib system in Paris was expanded to comprise 20,000 rental bikes parked in about 1,500 bicycle racks. In a very short time the Vélib bicycles have become a well-used service, primarily for short trips: 18 minutes on average. Here the idea is to enable many more or less experienced bicyclists acquainted with the locality to bicycle in a network that is neither very safe nor well developed. Although there have been a number of accidents, the program has had the valuable re-

The idea of offering bicycles to borrow or rent has spread rapidly (Lyon, France).

sult that more people now bicycle in Paris — on rental bikes and personal bikes. In only one year the number of trips on personal bicycles has doubled, an increase that has doubtless been inspired and reinforced by the bicycle traffic on the new Vélib bicycles. The Vélib bicycles accounted for one-third of all bicycle trips in Paris in 2008, and bicycles in total accounted for between 2% and 3% of all traffic in Paris.[27]

Inspired by the development in Paris, among other cities, many new city bicycle systems are underway at this time, also in cities that have essentially no bicycle infrastructure or bicycle culture. The idea seems to be that easily accessible city bikes can kick-start development of more bicycle cities on the principle that first you send people out on city bicycles and then you gradually develop comfortable, safe bicycle networks. There are good reasons to be cautious about sending inexperienced bicyclists out on two wheels in cities where bicycle traffic and networks do not have the critical mass to allow city bikes to reinforce ongoing development. Bicycle traffic and traffic safety must be taken seriously, and experiences from good bicycle cities incorporated, before experimenting with cheap bicycle campaigns. City bikes must be a link in efforts to build and reinforce bicycle culture — not the spearhead.

on the way to a new bicycle culture

A number of cities, particularly in Scandinavia, Germany and Holland have witnessed a considerable development in bicycle use in recent years. The number of bicyclists and bicycle trips grows gradually as it becomes more practical and safe to bicycle. Biking simply becomes the way to get around town. Bicycle traffic changes gradually from being a small group of death-defying bicycle enthusiasts to being a wide popular movement comprising all age groups and layers of society from members of Parliament and mayors to pensioners and school children.

Bicycle traffic changes character dramatically in the process. When there are many bicycles and many children and seniors among them, the tempo is more stately and safe for all parties. Racing bicycles and Tour de France gear is replaced by more comfortable family bicycles and ordinary clothing. Cycling moves from being a sport and test of survival to being a practical way to get around town — for everyone.

This shift in culture from fast slalom bicycle trips between cars and many infringements of traffic regulations to a law-abiding stream of children, young people and seniors bicycling in a well-defined bicycle network has a big impact on society's perception of bicycle traffic as a genuine alternative and reasonable supplement to other forms of transport. The shift in culture also brings bicycles more in line with pedestrians and city life in general, and is one more reason that bicycles have a natural place in this book about city life.

from car culture to bicycle culture

Cities are wonderfully innovative in their efforts to strengthen a broader bicycle culture and demonstrate that bicycles are an obvious choice for

In New York City 300 km/180 miles of new bicycle paths were built from 2007 to 2009. A comprehensive program to introduce the idea of bicycling to New Yorkers was instituted at the same time. Car free "summer streets" are arranged in the summer months, so that residents of the city can experience the delights of walking and bicycling in comfort (Park Avenue, Manhattan, summer 2009).

almost everyone. Schools offer intensive bicycle training, companies and institutions compete to have the highest percentage of bicyclists among their employees, and information campaigns, bicycle weeks and car-free days are held.

Many cities now open bicycle streets on Sunday in campaigns to develop bicycle culture. Sunday is a particularly good day for two reasons: car traffic is usually limited and people usually have more time for exercise and experiences. The idea of closing city streets to car traffic, turning them into temporary bicycle streets instead, has been popular in Central and South America for years. The extensive "Ciclovia" program in Bogotà, Columbia is one of the best known and best developed initiatives of this kind.

In the post-millennium years, the idea of reinforcing bicycle traffic has spread to more and more of those cities where cars have dominated planning for decades.

Ambitious strategies have been developed to establish extensive bicycle networks in the large Australian cities Melbourne and Sydney. Planners in both cities are hard at work laying out new bicycle lanes and moving existing lanes away from traffic and into safer "Copenhagen-style bicycle lanes" where bicycles move inside the rows of parked cars. New York City planners are working on a new traffic plan that will make NYC one of the world's most sustainable metropolises.

New York City's building density, flat terrain and wide streets provide good opportunities for converting car traffic to bicycle traffic, and a new bicycle network of 3,000 km/1,800 m of bike lanes is planned for the city's five boroughs: Manhattan, Bronx, Queens, Brooklyn and Staten Island. Work on the new bicycle lanes started in 2007 and already in the course of 2007 – 2008 about one-quarter of the planned bicycle lanes have been established and significant growth in bicycle traffic is evident. In New York the idea of closing streets to car traffic on Sundays, which NYC calls "summer streets" was introduced in 2008 as a popular link to the efforts to develop a new bicycle culture.

In future, concern about sustainability, climate change and health will most certainly mean that increasingly more cities, like New York City, will double their efforts to develop a new culture for city life and movement. Increased bicycle traffic is an obvious answer to many of the problems cities struggle with worldwide.

bicycles in economically
developing countries

Bicycle traffic already plays a key role in the overall traffic picture in many cities in economically developing countries. However, bicycle traffic is typically given poor and dangerous conditions. People bicycle by necessity, and individual mobility is often a prerequisite for being able to get to work and earn a living.

In many cities bicycles or bicycle rickshaws handle the lion's share of goods and people transport. Dhaka in Bangladesh has 12 million inhabit-

Bicycles play an important role for transport and mobility in many developing countries.

bicycle traffic and urban development — hindrance or opportunity?

ants, and the city's 400,000 bicycle rickshaws ensure cheap sustainable transport as well as providing a modest but vital income to upwards of one million people.

Many of the cities that actually have extensive bicycle traffic today unfortunately also have forces at work to reduce bicycle traffic in favor of more room for vehicular traffic.

In Dhaka, for example, bicycle taxis are considered a problem for the ongoing development of the city. Small motorcycles have replaced bicycles in many cities in Indonesia and Vietnam. Only a few decades ago, large Chinese cities were world famous for their volume of bicyclists, today bicycle traffic has in many cities almost disappeared from the street scene due to traffic reprioritization or even direct bans on bicycles.

In this category of cities, giving bicycle traffic a higher priority needs to be a key ingredient in a policy aimed to effectively utilize street space, reduce energy consumption and pollution, and provide mobility for the great majority of people who cannot afford cars. In addition, investing in bicycle infrastructure is affordable in comparison with other types of traffic investment.

bicycle policy as strategy for development and sustainability

New direction and reprioritizing of city policy is underway throughout the world. Fortunately, this includes prioritizing bicycle traffic in many cities in economically developing countries such as Mexico City and Bogota, Columbia, which will be described in chapter six.

5

Life, space, buildings
— in that order

Brasília Syndrome — urban planning from above and outside

From the air Brasília looks like a stylized eagle, with government buildings at the head and wings sheltering housing and institutions.

Brasília 1:250,000

n   20,000 ft

7,500 m

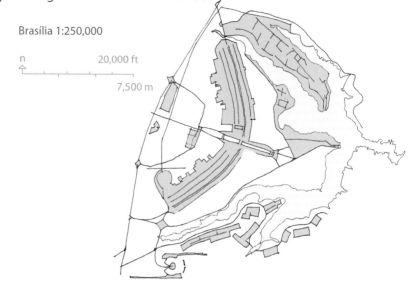

The government quarter precisely designed with tall buildings bordering a broad green area concluded by the Parliament building. An impressive sight — seen from a suitable distance.

The people landscape in Brasília is an abject failure. City space is too large and utterly uninviting, paths are too long, straight and uninteresting, and parked cars prevent pleasurable walking in the rest of the city.

The Brasília Syndrome

human landscape — the key to better cities for people

The previous chapter dealt with a number of requirements for the city at eye level, which means working with the smallest urban planning scale: the human landscape.

The reason for the extensive treatment of the small scale here is its general neglect by urban planners. Another cardinal point is that working with the small scale is the key to ensuring better conditions for the human dimension.

These same reasons are a compelling argument for why considerations about the small scale should become a carefully integrated part of city and development planning. However, reaching this goal will necessitate dramatic changes in habitual thinking and working methods.

city scale, site planning scale and human scale

Put simply, urban design and city planning can be described as work involving several very different levels of scale.

There is the large scale, which is holistic treatment of the city including quarters, functions and traffic facilities. This is the city as it is seen at a distance or from an aerial perspective.

Then there is the middle scale, the development scale, which describes how the individual segments or quarters of the city should be designed, and how buildings and city space are organized. This is city planning from a low-flying helicopter perspective.

Last but certainly not least is the small scale, the human landscape. This is the city as the people who will use city space experience it at eye level. It is not the large lines of the city or spectacular placement of buildings that are interesting here, but rather the quality of the human landscape as intuited by people walking and staying in the city. This is working with 5 km/h – 3 mph architecture.

good city planning requires coordinated work with all three scales

In practice, working with the three scales means operating with three very different disciplines, each with its own playing rules and quality criteria. Ideally all three levels of scale should be treated and amalgamated into a convincing whole that provides inviting space for people in the city.

The goal should be total treatment in which the city in its entirety — the skyline, placement of buildings and proportions of city space — are combined on the basis of careful treatment of space sequences, details and furnishing at eye level.

city planning — from above and
from the outside

In many cases, this ideal stands in contrast to a planning practice rooted in modernism, which focuses on buildings rather than holism and city space.

Photographs in which the client, mayor and proud architects stand bowed over the model of a new development illustrate the method and the problem. The development is being viewed from an aerial perspective a considerable distance above the model. From that height the elements of the development, the buildings, blocks and roads, can be moved around until the composition is in place and everything looks good — seen from above and from the outside.

The city viewed in helicopter perspective. Who is in charge of city life?

Planning cities and developments from above and from the outside typically means that only the two top-level scales — city scale and development scale — are properly addressed.

Many important decisions must be made on the city and site planning scales. On these two scales, a wealth of information as well as specific architectural programs are generally available as support. The most significant financial interests are also concentrated here, and highly specialized planners are available to handle problems on the basis of a large body of experience.

The situation is very different for the human scale, a difficult and rather intangible scale to work with. Both experience and relevant information tend to be scarce, which also means that there are seldom any useful architectural programs available in support. The financial interests tied to the two top-level scales are not as obvious either for the human landscape.

city life doesn't have a chance
with priorities ordered like this:
buildings, space, life

There are good rational explanations for why city planning starts from above and from the outside in many situations. Priorities are typically ordered like this: first the large outlines of the city, then the buildings and last the spaces in between. However, experience from decades of city planning shows that this method does not work for the human landscape and the desire to invite people to use city space. On the contrary: in almost all cases it has proved impossible to meet the goal of ensuring good conditions for city life if the majority of planning decisions are made on the top-level scale, and if work with city life is reduced to treating only those areas left over in the larger picture. Unfortunately, the conclusion is that the human dimension is sorely lacking in most new cities and developments.

the Brasília Syndrome — using
only the top-level scale

One of the most outstanding examples of modernistic city planning is Brasília, the capital of Brazil. Planned and developed in 1956 on the basis of Lúcio da Costa's winning project in an architectural competition, the city officially became Brazil's capital in 1960 and now has more than three million inhabitants. This new city gives us a good opportunity to assess the consequences of planning focused exclusively on the top-level scale: city and development planning.

Seen from the air, Brasília is a beautiful composition: designed like an eagle with the government quarters at the head and residential areas in the wings. The composition is still interesting in helicopter perspective, with distinct white government buildings and large housing blocks placed around large squares and green areas. So far, so good.

However, the city is a catastrophe seen at eye level, the scale planners ignored. City spaces are too large and amorphous, streets are too wide, and sidewalks and paths are too long and straight. The large green areas are crisscrossed by trampled footpaths showing how the inhabitants have voted with their feet in protest at the stiff, formal city plan. If you are not on an airplane or in a helicopter or car — and most people who live in Brasília are not — there is not much to rejoice about.

The Brasília Syndrome, where the two top-level scales are treated while the small scale is neglected, is unfortunately widespread as a planning principle.

The syndrome is at work in new housing developments in many parts of the world, for example, in China and other fast-growing regions in Asia. In Europe, too, many new urban quarters and developments are plagued by the Brasília Syndrome, particularly new areas near large cities, such as Oerestad on the outskirts of Copenhagen.

Dubai, where a very large number of introverted high-rises have been built within only a few years, represents another large urban area where efforts have concentrated on the large scale and spectacular constructions and not much else. Seen at eye level, there is not much to cheer about here.

City planning from above and outside. Interest is focused on buildings rather than spaces and holism (Oerestad, Copenhagen and Dubai).

5.2
Life, space, buildings
— in that order

the necessity of starting with life and waiting with buildings

If cities and buildings are going to invite people to come and stay, the human scale will require new and consistent treatment. Working with this scale is the most difficult and most sensitive urban planning discipline. If this work is neglected or fails, city life never stands a chance. The widespread practice of planning from above and outside must be replaced with new planning procedures from below and inside, following the principle: first life, then space, then buildings.

life, space, buildings
— in that order, please

Instead of the reverse order in the planning process that prioritizes buildings, then space and (perhaps) a little life, working with the human dimension requires life and space to be treated before buildings.

In brief, the method involves preparatory work that determines the character and extent of the anticipated life in the development. Then programs are prepared for the city spaces and city structure based on the desired walking and bicycling connections. Once the city space and connections are set, buildings can be positioned to ensure the best possible coexistence between life, spaces and buildings. From this point on, work expands into large developments and large districts, but is always rooted in the requirements for a well-functioning human scale.

Inherent in the order: life, space, buildings are opportunities for formulating requirements for new buildings early in the process to ensure that their functions and design support and enrich city space and city life.

The only successful approach to designing great cities for people must have city life and city space as a point of departure. It is the most important — and the most difficult approach, and it cannot be left until later in the process. If there is to be an order, it must start at eye level and end with a bird's-eye view. Naturally, the best of all worlds is to treat all three scales at the same time, holistically and convincingly.

traditional city planning based on city life and city space

The life-space-buildings order is not an innovation: what is new is modernism and modern drawing-board planning using the reverse order. Modernism has only held sway for a period of 60 or 70 years, precisely the period in which the human dimension has been seriously neglected.

The history of urban development shows how the oldest settlements were developed along paths, trails and market places.

Traders set up their tents and booths along the most popular paths in order to offer their wares to passersby. More permanent buildings re-

Monpazier 1:10,000

n
1,000 ft

300 m

The city plan of Monpazier (1283) in the south of France is based on gates, squares and streets. Distinctive arches line the square and provide the transition to main streets.

The life-space-buildings principle in action: the city plan for Adelaide in South Australia was drawn up in 1837 with emphasis on city space and parks, while buildings came later.

placed tents and booths, and towns with houses, streets and squares grew in a gradual process. The original paths and market places that were the starting point for city development have left traces in many modern cities. These old, organic cities tell the story of urban development from a human landscape at eye level to more complex structures.

For example, planning followed the life-space-buildings principles in areas that needed new towns such as the Greek and Roman colonies and in planned medieval towns like Monpazier in the south of France, founded in 1283. Urban planning in later years was also influenced by these principles. In the cities of the Renaissance and the Baroque periods, city space was primarily the starting point for planning, and the same principles can be found in many planned colonial towns in North and South America, such as Philadelphia, Pennsylvania (1681) and Savan-

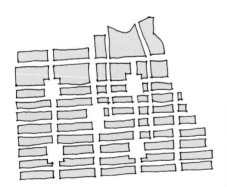

Adelaide 1:50,000

n
4,000 ft

1,500 m

nah, Georgia (1733), both in the USA. Adelaide in South Australia is another planned colony town that uses city space as the starting point for development. In Colonel William Light's plan from 1837, Adelaide was given a grid-pattern street network with five distinctive centrally located squares and a large green sward surrounding the entire town. Buildings were later constructed along the streets and squares in a gradual process. In even later periods, such as Berlage's urban developments in central Amsterdam (1917), common city space was the point of departure for city planning.

Thus the life-space-buildings order can be followed throughout urban history until the recent modernistic period in which buildings took center stage rather than life and space.

life, space, buildings
— a timeless concept

Throughout the period in which the Brasília Syndrome has dominated urban planning, fortunately there have also been isolated cases of urban districts and developments built in accordance with all three scales, with carefully treated holistic results to follow. Architect Ralph Erskine demonstrated the many advantages of treating the small scale and the other scales together: for example, his developments in Sweden: Tibro (1956 – 59), Landskrona (1970), Sandviken (1973 – 78) and in the UK in Newcastle upon Tyne (1973 – 78). Similarly, in the years after 1979, the New Urbanism movement endeavored to set development principles that carefully integrate the small scale. The Seaside resort in southern Florida is an illustration of these principles, although the life it supports represents only a very small part of modern, diverse city life. Like many other developments with the same point of departure, it is too isolated and the population density too low for it to work convincingly.

A city space plan was the first element in the planning of a new district south of Stockholm, Skarpnäck (1981 – 86). Gates, boulevards, squares, streets and parks were plotted first, and then architects were asked to design houses along the planned city spaces.
Right: original sketch for the city lay out by architect Klas Tham.

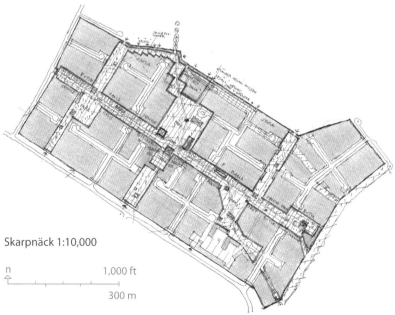

Skarpnäck 1:10,000

n

1,000 ft

300 m

Bo01 1:10,000

n
1,000 ft
300 m

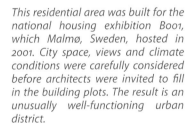

This residential area was built for the national housing exhibition Bo01, which Malmø, Sweden, hosted in 2001. City space, views and climate conditions were carefully considered before architects were invited to fill in the building plots. The result is an unusually well-functioning urban district.

Ralph Erskine's early Swedish projects inspired two interesting new developments that demonstrate the potential in planning ordered under the life, space, buildings principle.

Skarpnäck is a new urban area built in the years from 1981 to 1986 south of Stockholm. The area houses some 10,000 inhabitants. The urban plan represents a clear break with previous decades of planning in the region, which focused on placing individual buildings between traffic systems. Rather this plan shows the extent, position and dimensions of common space in the new urban area and provides guidelines on how future buildings should be placed and designed in support.

Development Bo01 in Malmø, Sweden (2001) was built on similar principles. The urban plan was developed by Professor Klas Tham, based on experience from previous work with Skarpnäck and several of Ralph Erskine's other developments. Bo01 too exemplifies careful work with city space, with focus on the proportions of spatial sequences as well as climate protection, with large buildings sheltering lower buildings. Care was also given to ensuring variation by using many different contractors and architects.

life, space and buildings in new developments

The new town of Almere (1976 – 1986) near Amsterdam in the Netherlands features rather narrow buildings and vertical integration, with housing consistently located on top of active ground-floor functions.

Soft edges for residential streets is one of the visionary, green city planning principles used in Vauban (1993 – 2006), a new part of town in Freiburg, in the south of Germany.

Life, space and buildings are the order of the day for new developments being built to gradually replace temporary dwellings near Cape Town, South Africa.

The waterfront in Vancouver, Canada, has low street-side buildings backed by tall narrow towers of apartments recessed on the property.

The result is a development with an unusual number of qualities that have made the area popular as a residential area as well as a destination for the entire city and region. Boo1 is a good place to live because the regional tourist destinations, waterfront spaces and local outdoor space have been carefully separated. There is room for everything.

These Swedish developments demonstrate that the human landscape, development and city plan can be treated holistically by paying careful attention to all scales.

a fine city with tall buildings on top: example Vancouver, Canada

In recent years Vancouver has carried out corresponding treatments of the city's various scales in a combined process. The extensive new development along the city's waterfront needed to meet two key requirements: high building density and good urban qualities in the streets of the new urban areas. The problem of ensuring many square meters and good qualities at eye level resulted in a careful design of the development in two layers. The lower level is two to four stories high, a plateau that follows building lines along the city streets. Above this plateau rise densely built skyscrapers recessed from the lines of the street, so that they do not impact on the pedestrian landscape. The skyscrapers are designed as slender towers to avoid shielding the waterfront view from the buildings behind, as well as to reduce the well-known impact of wind and shade on the streets below. All in all, Vancouver's plateau developments provide an interesting new orientation in attempts to combine large and small scales in the same development. Vancouver's new building is an inspiring contribution to the debate and dreams on creating great cities at eye level while still ensuring high building density.

good cities at eye level — a new subject for schools of architecture

So there are interesting international examples of how the requirement for high building density can be combined with concern for the human landscape. Finding the balance is key to establishing lively, safe, sustain-

now and again almost everything works: Granville Island, Vancouver

Granville Island 1:10,000

n
1,000 ft
300 m

Mixed function was the guiding principle for the conversion of a partially abandoned industrial area on Granville Island, Vancouver, into a new city park/quarter in the 1970s.

Schools, a theater, shops and housing were built alongside still-functioning industries. Granville Island is one of the few places in the world where almost all of the principles discussed in this book have been put into practice.

1. *Types of traffic were mixed in the original industrial quarter and still are today.*
2. *Market hall.*
3. *It is a principle for all ground floors to be active and transparent.*
4. *Another design principle is to maintain the character of the old industrial quarter. Buildings, city furniture and signs reflect the industrial history of the area.*

able and healthy cities. Some problems can be solved through the careful planning of cities and site plans, but it is crucial for the architecture, which is the point of departure for the individual buildings, to contribute directly to the quality at eye level.

The issue of how to make sure we have great cities at eye level should be treated as an important architectural challenge, to a far greater extent than it is in current practice. It was not that long ago that architecture did focus carefully on the design of buildings at street level. A smaller, more detailed scale was used where building met city. In turn, walking in cities was a rich, intense and multifaceted sensory experience thanks to the architectural care lavished on ground floors.

Modernism introduced new ideals. From the ground floor to the very top, buildings were typically constructed of identical materials with the same level of detail. Buildings were led directly down to the sidewalk from the height of five or ten or even forty stories. Now that the consequences of this mechanical treatment of the city's buildings are well recognized, surely it is time once again to put the special situation of ground floors on the agenda.

The demand for great cities at eye level, with taller buildings on top, necessitates a rediscovery of ground-floor architecture as a special discipline.

Don't ask what the city can do for your building, but what your building can do for the city! An obvious immediate response to this challenge could be: attractive ground floors that protrude a good piece away from the stories above.

Active lower floors with taller recessed building on top (Hobart, Australia).

These Copenhagen row houses look boring and uniform seen from the air. However, seen at eye level the row houses have so many qualities and function so convincingly that the city's largest concentration of architects and their families live here (Copenhagen, Denmark).

if only the little scale works well…

In addition to the projects in which large and small scales have been treated together, there are a surprising number of well-functioning developments that only give careful treatment to the small scale.

From very high up as well as from rooftops, the Copenhagen neighborhoods with modest building society row houses (1873 – 89) look uniform and boring. In street after street, the almost identical houses stand in low, even rows. There is not much to write home about — seen from a helicopter perspective.

However, down at eye level these row houses have qualities. Street space is carefully dimensioned, there are front gardens and landscaping, good space creation, great variation in details, good traffic safety and

The small scale always rates careful attention in situations where the number of visitors has economic impact. Disneyland in Paris, France, has no special aerial appeal, but down at eye level the entertainment park functions to perfection. To reinforce the good, inviting atmosphere, the upper stories of the buildings are reduced to 80% of ordinary size.

good climate. In brief, they fill almost all the requirements for a good human landscape, and residents are so busy exploiting their options that they scarcely have time to think that from the outside and above, their development looks uniform and boring.

Experience from developments like this underscores the fact that if one or more urban planning scales must be neglected, under no circumstances can it be the small scale: the human landscape.

It is also interesting that a development like this one, where the quality of the small scale is convincing, is among the city's most sought after and most expensive. Here too is where the largest concentration of architects and their families live: evidently architects know very well how they want to live.

The Free State of Christiania in Copenhagen is another example of how the careful treatment of the human landscape is an important prerequisite for the community's ability to function as a car-free area and alternative social model.

the small scale — a factor that determines where people will be invited

That the quality of the small scale is decisive for the life and attractiveness of an area is underscored by the careful attention paid to the human landscape in amusement parks, exhibition sites, market places and holiday resorts. What they have in common is offering good conditions to visitors — at eye level. The bird's eye view and helicopter perspective don't play much of a role here, and for good reason.

life, space, buildings — in existing cities

The working method that makes life in city space the object of special targeted focus is equally important in improving existing urban areas.

Typically the human landscape in cities has been neglected for years, often as a direct result of prioritizing car traffic. Gradually almost all cities

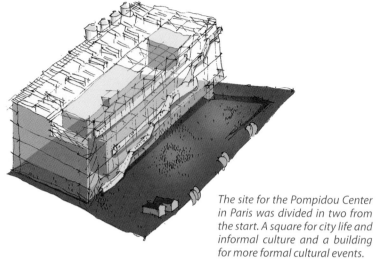

The site for the Pompidou Center in Paris was divided in two from the start. A square for city life and informal culture and a building for more formal cultural events.

In contrast to the Guggenheim Museum in Bilbao, Spain, which is closed on all sides (above), this Melbourne museum (above left) was designed to frame a very attractive city space (Federation Square, Melbourne, Australia).

The new opera house in Oslo, Norway, erases the boundaries between city and building. Roof surfaces were designed as city space that invites people for urban mountain climbing.

have established traffic departments that calculate the amount of traffic and assess parking conditions year after year. They collect data and make prognoses, traffic models and impact analyses, and in the process cars have become more and more visible and omnipresent in urban planning.

In contrast, it is rare that anyone has kept an eye on what has happened to city life and pedestrians. Life in the city has been taken for granted for decades. It is just something that has always been there, and the impact of steady deterioration has seldom been studied.

Whereas car traffic has typically become more visible in planning processes, the people activities in the cities have become more and more invisible.

Priorities need to be reordered here too. City life must be made visible and treated on the same level as other urban functions. Life must be prioritized, also in existing cities.

making life in the cities visible

Planning in new urban areas must start with expectations and prognoses about future activity patterns. In existing urban areas, one obvious starting point would be to study city life as it actually exists and then use this information to make plans for where and how to reinforce city life.

city life studies in Copenhagen
— for the past 40 years

Regular public space public life studies were introduced in Copenhagen in 1968, and over the years they have proven to be a highly valuable tool for the future planning of city space and improvements in the human landscape. The methods were originally developed as part of a research project at the School of Architecture, Royal Danish Academy of Fine Arts.

Put simply the methods involve mapping and assessing city space and registering the city life that takes place there. Typically urban life registration brings to light the extent of pedestrian and staying activities at selected times and days in various seasons of the year. This is a simple and inexpensive way to capture a relatively precise overview of how the spaces function and which activities take place.

Using precisely the same methods, the studies can be repeated at a later date such as two, five or ten years later, to show developments and changes in the way the city is used. Where traffic has been rerouted and city space improvements made, the effect of the changes can be read rather simply. In short, the methods make it possible to follow and develop life in the city.[1] In Copenhagen, public space public life studies have developed into a key planning tool that makes it possible for politicians and urban planners to acquire knowledge about how the city is changing, as well as to get ideas about how the city can be further improved.

Life in the city becomes visible, and over the years it has been a decisive factor for carrying out the many qualitative improvements of Copenhagen's public space.

City life studies conducted using identical registration methods provide a valuable opportunity to compare activity levels and behavior patterns in cities in different parts of the world.[2]
Pedestrian traffic on a summer weekday between 8 am and 10 pm.
Wellington and Stockholm between 10 am and 6 pm.

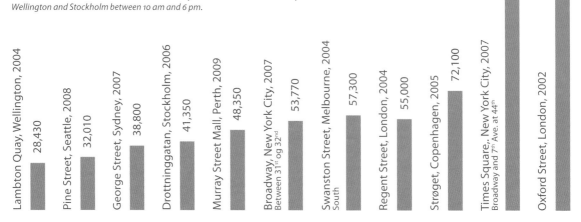

Lambton Quay, Wellington, 2004	Pine Street, Seattle, 2008	George Street, Sydney, 2007	Drottninggatan, Stockholm, 2006	Murray Street Mall, Perth, 2009	Broadway, New York City, 2007 Between 31st og 32nd	Swanston Street, Melbourne, 2004 South	Regent Street, London, 2004	Strøget, Copenhagen, 2005	Times Square, New York City, 2007 Broadway and 7th Ave. at 44th	Oxford Street, London, 2002
28,430	32,010	38,800	41,350	48,350	53,770	57,300	55,000	72,100	137,400	139,230

city life studies as a universal planning tool

Although the value of systematic studies of city life as a tool for establishing city space policy and city space planning was first demonstrated in Copenhagen in 1968, today it is taken for granted that urban planners consider data on city life on an equal footing with data on traffic.

In the years that followed the initial research project, city life studies as a planning tool have been further developed through studies of urban renewal projects in cities of widely different character in various parts of the world and in dramatically different climate regions.

City life has been studied in urban conglomerates varying in size from small provincial towns to large cities like London (2004) and New York (2007 – 2009). This list of cities where the methods have been used in the past two decades gives an indication of the variation in geography and cultures: Europe (Oslo, Norway, Stockholm, Sweden, Riga, Latvia and Rotterdam, Holland), Africa (Cape Town, South Africa), Middle East (Amman, Jordan), Australasia (Perth, Adelaide, Melbourne, Sydney and Brisbane, Australia, Wellington and Christchurch, New Zealand) and North America (Seattle, Washington and San Francisco, California).[3]

The work in many different cities has provided a detailed picture of the character and extent of city life there for use in local urban planning. In a larger context, the studies have provided a valuable overview of the cultural patterns and development trends in various parts of the world. Having data from various cities has also made it possible to carry out comparisons and ensure the transfer of knowledge, inspiration and solutions from city to city.

life in city space has become visible

The methods used to study city life have developed and become more refined in a gradual process. In many cities the various attempts to systematize information about city life have now been developed into fixed

City life studies are usually conducted by manual registration, which gives observers the necessary data as well as first-hand knowledge of how city space functions.

Registration showing average levels of staying activities in Copenhagen city space a summer weekday between noon and 4 pm.[4]

- Commercial activity
- Cultural activity
- Standing
- Secondary seating
- Café seating
- Bench seating

888
270
240
154
338
384
203
140
248
342
74
102
161
119

n
2,000 ft
Copenhagen 1:25,000
750 m

procedures, with city life developments studied regularly as the starting point for city policy discussions and setting targets. And now after many years of neglect, work on the human dimension in city policy has tools and planning practice in support.

first life, then space, then buildings — as a universal requirement for urban planners

Just as the experiences from planning new developments underscore the necessity of treating life, space and buildings in that order, the experiences from existing cities and urban areas indicate that city life must be made visible and awarded priority in planning processes.

First life, then space and then buildings have the character of a universal requirement for planning processes in the 21st century.

An extensive city life study was conducted in Perth, Australia, in 1993. Many city space improvements have been made since then and a 2009 study showed that the activity level in the city had doubled. Photos show sidewalk scenes before and after city space improvements.

6

Developing cities

a crucial issue in all parts of the world

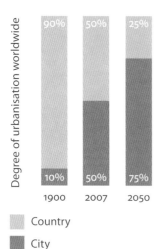

Degree of urbanisation worldwide

1900	2007	2050
90%	50%	25%
10%	50%	75%

Country

City

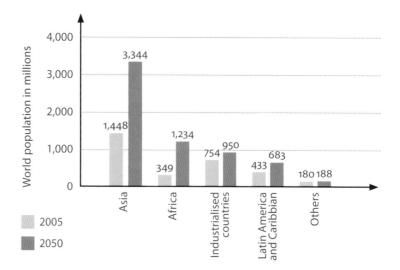

World population in millions

4,000

3,000

2,000

1,000

0

Asia 1,448 / 3,344

Africa 349 / 1,234

Industrialised countries 754 / 950

Latin America and Caribbian 433 / 683

Others 180 / 188

2005

2050

Above: More than half of the world population now lives in cities, and the percentage is expected to rise to 75% before 2050.[1] Above right: Expected population development in cities worldwide: 2005 – 2050.[2]

Throughout history city space has served as meeting place, marketplace and connection space, and most of the world's cities still provide the framework for these vital functions (market day, Chichicastenango, Guatemala).

In many cities, increased traffic has exerted heavy pressure on the traditional functions of city space (Amman, Jordan).

the human dimension — a crucial issue in all parts of the world

There are strong arguments for prioritizing humanistic urban planning that carefully accommodates the people who use city space. Invitations to walk, bicycle and take part in city life should certainly comprise cities everywhere regardless of level of economic development.

A number of conditions underscore and reinforce the importance of working with the human dimension of urban planning in the rapidly growing cities in developing countries.

most people now live in cities and cities are growing explosively

Within a century, the total world population has grown at lightening speed from 1.65 billion people in about 1900 to six billion in 2000, and growth is expected to reach nine billion by 2050.[3]

Much of this dramatic growth is seen in urban areas. In 1900 ten percent of the world population lived in cities. By the year 2007 that share had swollen to 50%, and it is expected that 75% of the world population will be urban by 2050.[4]

overpopulation and poverty make common urban space all the more precious

The rapid rise in the urban populations of developing countries is the catalyst for many problems and challenges.

In many regions the problem of housing so many new urban dwellers has resulted in the spread of large informal housing areas that are densely populated, primitively constructed and lack almost all forms of

When motorized traffic does not dominate, the traditional functions of city space as meeting place, marketplace and connection space continue in balance (hutong in Beijing, China).

In many developing countries, numerous important daily functions take place outdoors in city space. Culture, climate and economic conditions ensure that life in city space has great impact on the living conditions and life quality in these cities (TV on Zanzibar, Tanzania, street trade, Dhaka, Bangladesh, and hairdresser, Hanoi, Vietnam).

services. The pressure on cities also leads to the overpopulation of existing housing areas, which overpowers utilities, traffic systems and, of course, common space and parks. In addition, new housing complexes featuring high-rise, dense construction are being built at record speed near large cities, and here common space is usually under-dimensioned and poor in quality.

A common feature of most urban inhabitants of cities in developing countries is their very modest living standard. It is precisely in those housing areas with a high population density and few economic resources that outdoor space has a particularly large bearing on living conditions. Where possible, many ordinary activities are conducted outside near dwellings, on streets, squares or any other common grounds.

In many regions, culture, tradition and climate have dictated an extensive and multifaceted outdoor life that always has and still does play an important role in living conditions and life quality. In these cities in particular it is important to ensure the future availability of enough well-functioning free space: parks, squares and opportunities for expression in existing and new urban districts.

strong arguments for maintaining and reinforcing pedestrian and bicycle traffic

Along with the need for economic development and transport over greater distances to new types of workplaces, rapid urban growth and large concentrations of urban dwellers mean unconscionable pressure on the traffic infrastructure.

While access to cars and motorized transport will increase gradually, for now the great majority of inhabitants have very limited or no access to cars and motorcycles. Public transport is typically weakly developed, expensive and slow.

Traditionally walking or bicycling has played a great role in mobility for these population groups, and a large share of urban dwellers con-

Many new residential areas are built according to principles and ideologies that give very low priority to outdoor activities (Beijing, China).

bicycle rickshaws in Dhaka, Bangladesh

About 400,000 bicycle rickshaws offer cheap and sustainable transport to the 12 million inhabitants of Dhaka, Bangladesh. The rickshaw business is thought to provide a living to upwards of one million people. Discussions on how to deal with car traffic often stand on the argument that the bicycle rickshaws "are in the way of progress." Unfortunately, conflicts of this type are common in many economically developing countries.[5]

tinue to rely on walking, bicycling or using public transport options. However, increased motorization dramatically reduces opportunities to walk and bicycle, and while some groups do become more mobile, even larger groups find themselves less mobile and perhaps without any real options for getting around. There are unusually strong and compelling arguments for providing good conditions for walking and bicycling safely and comfortably to the inhabitants of rapidly growing cities in developing countries. Naturally the development of walking and bicycling options should not be seen as a temporary measure for the poorest members of the population. Rather it is a proactive and general investment in improving living conditions and developing sustainable transport systems to reduce pollution and traffic risk, and accommodate all groups of society. In these cities too, good walking and biking systems are an important prerequisite for having effective public traffic systems.

economic growth and declining
life quality

In general the rapidly growing cities in developing countries have a number of common features. Their traditional traffic of pedestrians and bicycles is declining and rapidly growing motorized traffic is filling cities to the bursting point. Parallel with signs of economic growth in many cities, particularly in Asia, is a reduction in life quality.

Cars and motorcycles are grid-locked in endless traffic snarls, transport time increases for everyone, and problems with noise, air pollution and traffic accidents grow day by day.

Conditions for pedestrians and the remaining stalwart bicyclists have been intolerable for a long time, but they are accepted out of necessity. Pedestrians push their way through those crowded sidewalks that haven't been dismantled or overtaken by parking, or they walk out on the street with their baskets, bags and children, while bicyclists weave in and out of traffic.

Traditional outdoor life featuring handcrafts, street exhibitions, street trade on sidewalks and street kitchens and small eateries along buildings is also under pressure. Every day space is reduced in favor of parking and traffic, and every kind of outdoor activity in city space is negatively impacted by noise, pollution and insecurity. Free space is built on, parks are converted into parking places and play opportunities simply disappear. Every day the situation is a little worse than it was the day before.

It can be stated matter-of-factly that the dramatic development of traffic has meant a marked reduction in opportunities for expression and life quality for large groups of the population, especially the economically poorest groups.

In contrast to this general picture of growing cities whose problems multiply by the day, it is inspiring to see examples of city policies showcasing visionary politicians and planners who are looking for new solutions

Only a few years ago, Vietnam's cities were dominated by bicycle traffic. Today, however, those bicycle cities have been taken over by motorbikes. Motorized transport provides improved mobility for some groups in society but creates numerous new problems concerning city quality.

Rapid urban growth in Curitiba, Brazil, has been concentrated in linear growth corridors along the city's new bus boulevards. Rapid bus transport on its own bus lanes has later been the inspiration for many cities.

innovative thinking about urban growth and transport: Curitiba, Brazil

to some of their most pressing problems. Naturally they hone in on traffic solutions, but they also make a targeted effort to reinforce city life and improve opportunities to walk and bicycle as a link in overall policies to generally enhance economic potential, urban quality and living conditions.

In recent decades, numerous cities have established new metro, train and light rail systems. However, these systems require substantial investments and often take years to establish. A number of cities have turned instead to BRT: Bus Rapid Transport. These "metro rubber wheel" solutions are interesting because they are cheap and simple to establish, yet can transport large numbers of passengers quickly and comfortably through the city.

Curitiba, a city undergoing powerful development in southern Brazil, has shown a true pioneering spirit in the transport arena. In the period from 1965 to 2000 the city's population grew from 500,000 to 1,500,000 and it continues to grow. Starting in 1965, urban growth has been organized around five large bus streets spread out like fingers from the middle of the city. Large articulated buses service these streets. Purpose-built bus stops that allow passengers to get on and off quickly and green lights for buses at every intersection keep traffic moving.

Two other key elements in Mayor Jamie Lehrner's visionary city plan are short, convenient paths to and from buses and bicycle access on bus streets. A large number of newly established parks and a comprehensive system of car-free streets and squares in the city center ensure free space and opportunities for expression in this rapidly growing city.

All in all Curitiba is a model for how to provide good conditions for pedestrian and bicycle traffic and prioritize other aspects of city life despite economic challenges and a rapidly growing populace.

innovative thinking about city quality and social sustainability: Bogota, Colombia

Bogota, Colombia, a South American city of six million inhabitants, has carried out remarkable city planning from 1995 to the present. Particularly in the years from 1998 to 2001 under the leadership of Mayor Enrique Penalosa, work to improve city quality has been a high priority. In a city where only 20% of the inhabitants owned a car, for years the bulk of transport investment was devoted to improving car traffic.

Starting in 1998 priorities were changed to improving mobility and living conditions for the remaining 80% of the population. Residents

An extensive BRT (Bus Rapid Transport) system was introduced in Bogota, Colombia, in 1999. Like in Curitiba, the transmillenio buses in Bogota drive in their own bus lanes and offer considerably faster transport through the city than a car driver could ever hope to manage on the overfilled roads.

An important element in the urban renovation work in Bogata, Colombia has been to ensure better conditions for pedestrians and bicyclists. Sidewalks were improved in many city streets and new pedestrian and bicycle paths were laid through the city's green belts as well as out to new residential areas.

without automobiles needed to be able to walk, bicycle and use effective means of public transport to get around the city.

A program was implemented to improve the conditions for pedestrian and bicycle traffic. Blocked by parked cars for years, sidewalks were cleared and renovated, and 330 km/200 miles of new bicycle paths were built. Bicycles were considered a practical and cheap means of transport that would ensure increased mobility for the inhabitants of the poorest districts in the city. And in connection with building new city neighborhoods, good pedestrian and bicycle paths were established as a matter of course before roads for vehicular traffic.

Like in Curitiba, a key element in overall planning in Bogota was the introduction of an extensive BRT bus system with dedicated bus lanes throughout the city. The transmillenio bus system, introduced around the year 2000, has radically reduced the time it takes to cross town. The overall planning objective was to support the economic and social development of the city by providing better conditions and mobility to the least privileged inhabitants. If it is easier to walk and bicycle and faster to use public transport, then it is also considerably simpler to get to workplaces in all parts of the city. The transmillenio buses have an average speed of 29,1 km/h (18 mph) right past traffic congestion, and the system is used daily by 1,4 million passengers. On average each passenger gains 300 hours annually, hours that used to be spent in traffic, but which can now be spent on more effective work time as well as more time at home with the family.

Overall planning did not neglect recreational options. In only a few years 900 new parks and squares have been built, particularly in densely populated areas where dwellings are small and the need for free space correspondingly great.[6]

City planners in many large cities in economically developing and de-

"Ciclovia" in Bogota, Colombia. Every Sunday between 7 am and 2 pm, 120 km/75 miles of the city's streets are closed to cars and opened for bicycling and playing in the street. Over the years the Ciclovia has become very popular and on an ordinary Sunday more than one million people come out on the city's streets to walk, bicycle, meet and greet.

veloped countries alike have been inspired by the examples of Curitiba and Bogota to implement urban improvements and social programs. Particularly the principles of prioritized BRT bus systems have been further developed in among others Jakarta, Guatemala City, Guangzhou, Istanbul, Mexico City, Brisbane and Los Angeles.

The introduction of special bicycle streets on weekends — la ciclovia — is another initiative applied in Bogota. The idea now has worldwide adherents and is used in many cities. Using the ciclovia model, a number of city streets are closed to car traffic on Sunday, where less space is needed to handle the traffic volume. Instead the streets are converted to bicycle streets and playgrounds, where city dwellers can get fresh air, exercise, teach their children to bicycle and in general enjoy the advantages of bicycling in the city. Every Sunday morning Bogota closes off 120 km/75 miles of city streets to car traffic. In time, the ciclovia has developed into something of a street party with more than one million participants every week.

In recent years, numerous other cities have adopted the obvious idea of using city streets as car-free pedestrian and bicycle streets on weekends. In 2008, New York introduced its first "summer streets," and various other American cities, which are also working to develop a bicycle culture, have subsequently taken up the idea.

Under the years of apartheid rule in South Africa, the nonwhite inhabitants were banished to townships outside cities. Townships like this one near Cape Town are known for their population density, poor building quality and crushing poverty.

Improving conditions in the townships is high on the political agenda. Public space used for everyday activities has been selected as an obvious area for fast and widespread improvements (Cape Town, South Africa).

dignified places programme in Cape Town, South Africa

In the many cases where it will take a long time and many resources to implement extensive city improvements, it is important to be able to carry out minor projects quickly and cheaply to reinforce daily life, provide inspiration and serve as a start in individual housing areas. This is the background for the "dignified places programme" campaign carried out from the year 2000 in Cape Town South Africa by city planners under the leadership of architect Barbara Southworth.

The transition from apartheid rule to democracy in 1994 provided the incentive for a major campaign to improve life quality for the inhabitants of the city's many impoverished townships. However, the funds available only allowed a few selected improvement projects to be carried out. Top priority was given to establishing access to water and building sewers as well as to initiating a program to establish good quality city space in poor neighborhoods.

One feature of the townships was that they had spaces in front of the school, bus station, intersection or sports hall that served as a social hub and city space. Although typically these city spaces were weakly defined sites, dusty and neglected, devoid of furniture or landscaping, they were important and well-visited meeting places. This is where a vital part of community activities took place. Improving this space would improve the framework for daily activities as well as demonstrating that now, after many years of repression, it was once again possible to meet and speak in common city space.

Making extensive use of local artists and craftsmen, so far it has been possible to carry out more than 40 city space projects to bring dignity, beauty and utility to various quarters. Every city space has been de-

dignified places programme in Cape Town, South Africa

The Guga S'thebe Art Centre in Langa, Cape Town.

Lansdowne Corner project in Philippi, Cape Town. The porticos provide shade and mark the placement for market traders.

New public space in front of the train station in Philippi. Market stalls along the square provide services for the neighborhood and the many train passengers (Cape Town, South Africa).

signed specifically for the individual site, but their shared features include good furniture and pavements, shade trees, and pergola systems to define booths for street traders. Other trade takes place in converted containers placed to demarcate space. In time these space-defining walls will hold the service facilities to be built around new squares.[7]

Throughout the history of human settlements development has begun by building around well-used paths and sites. Later came market stalls for traders then buildings were erected and later still more complex urban constructions. Cities started with life and key city spaces, and Cape Town is no exception. Here too the plan is to continue improving poor quarters according to these principles. Establishing "dignified places" where dignity and meeting places are most needed is certainly a good place to start. And an inspiring strategy to emulate.

modest efforts
— with a great pay off

Together the rapid urban growth of the world's largest and poorest cities represents an enormous complex of problems. Housing, jobs, health, transport, education and utilities are needed. Pollution must be combated, garbage removed, and living conditions generally improved.

In the face of the challenge of dealing with so many sectors in only a short time and with limited means, it is important as well as reasonable to ensure that the human dimension of city planning is carefully integrated into work on city development.

While the desire of many people to have access to cars or motorcycles in connection with economic growth is understandable and respected, the move towards more motorized traffic should not be accepted at the expense of traditional modes of transport: walking and bicycling. In many cities in the economically developed part of the world, notably in Denmark and the Netherlands, good examples exist showing motorized traffic and people traffic moving side by side. The need for this type of reasonable coexistence between street uses is even more urgent in developing cities. Compared to all other areas of investment, the funds needed to provide for the human dimension will be minor indeed.

The main investment will be to show respect and concern with regard to incorporating the human dimension in all forms of urban projects. Crucial improvements in living conditions, happiness and dignity for the many new inhabitants can be ensured for small means.

Thoughtfulness, concern and empathy are the most important ingredients.

global unity — concerning problems and solutions

Although the problems of cities in various parts of the world and at different levels of economic development are not all alike, the differences involved in incorporating the human dimension in city planning are actually minor. The same pattern appears everywhere, namely that for the past 50 years, the human dimension has been seriously neglected in connection with urban development.

In economically developed cities neglect owes largely to planning ideologies, rapid motorization and difficulties in switching from a model in which life in cities was an obvious part of tradition to a model where city life needs the active support of careful planning. In rapidly growing cities in developing countries, population growth, burgeoning economic opportunities and explosive development in traffic have created monumental problems in city streets.

Whereas neglect has just about extinguished city life in some economically developed countries, pressure from developments has pushed city life into extremely adverse conditions in many countries with less developed economies. In both cases making city life viable will require careful work with people's conditions for walking, bicycling and using the city's outdoor space.

basically it is all about respect for people

Core issues are respect for people, dignity, zest for life and the city as meeting place. In these areas, the differences between the dreams and desires of people in various parts of the world are not dramatic. The methods for dealing with these issues are also surprisingly similar, because it all comes down to people, who have the same basic point of departure. All people have walking, a sensory apparatus, movement options and basic behavior patterns in common. To a far greater extent than we know it today, city planning must start with people in future. It is cheap, simple, healthy and sustainable to build cities for people — as well as an obvious policy for meeting the challenges of the 21st century. It is high time that we rediscover the human dimension in city planning — in all parts of the world.

"to be a good architect you have to love people"

In an interview in 2000, architect Ralph Erskine was asked what it takes to become a good architect. He responded: "To be a good architect you have to love people, because architecture is an applied art and deals with the frameworks for people's lives."[8] It is really as simple as that.

7

Toolbox

Working carefully to assemble people and events is also an important prerequisite for developing city life in new urban areas (BoO1 [2001], Malmø, Sweden)

Planning principles: to assemble or disperse

Several general city planning principles make up a crucial prerequisite for working with the human dimension. Five of these principles are illustrated here. The first four principles deal primarily with quantity and about ensuring that people and events are assembled in built-up areas; the fifth principle is on improving the quality of city space in order to invite people to spend more time.

1. Carefully locate the city´s functions to ensure shorter distances between them and a critical mass of people and events.

2. Integrate various functions in cities to ensure versatility, wealth of experience, social sustainability and a feeling of security in individual city districts.

3. Design city space so it is inviting and safe for pedestrian and bicycling traffic.

4. Open up the edges between the city and buildings so that life inside buildings and outside in city spaces can work together.

5. Work to strengthen the invitations to invite longer stays in city space because a few people spending much time in a place provide the same sense of lively space as many people spending only a short time. Of all the principles and methods available for reinforcing life in cities, inviting people to spend more time is the simplest and most effective.

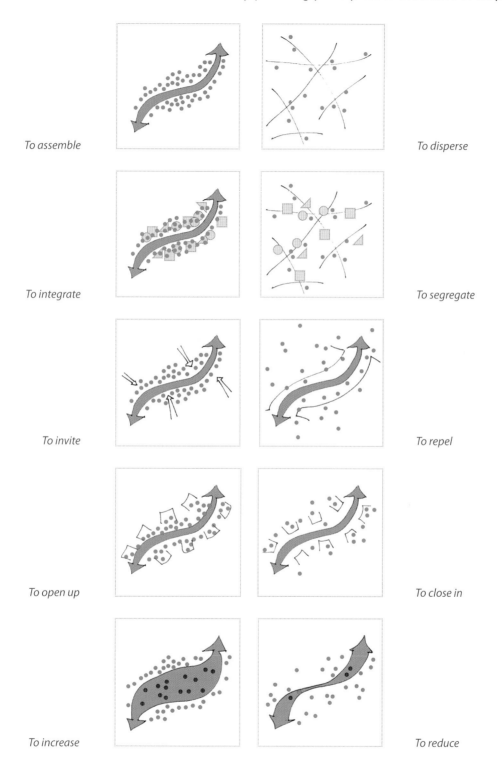

To assemble

To disperse

To integrate

To segregate

To invite

To repel

To open up

To close in

To increase

To reduce

Source: Jan Gehl, Life Between Buildings *(1971), 6th edition, The Danish Architectural Press, 2010.*
Further developed: Gehl Architects — Urban Quality Consultants, 2009.

In 2007, New Road in Brighton, UK, was converted from an ordinary traffic street to a pedestrian priority street. The street is now used for many different activities and has far more users than before (also see page 15).

Four traffic planning principles

In the 1960s and 1970s , when the car invasion gathered speed, basically only two types of streets, traffic streets and pedestrian streets, existed. In this same period in many new built-up areas, road systems were established in accordance with the idea of segregating car traffic and pedestrian/bicycle traffic into completely separate traffic systems. While the idea was terrific in theory, it was almost always problematic in practice, because human traffic as a general rule chooses the shortest routes. In addition, separate path systems often led to safety and security issues in the evening and at night.

In subsequent years, particularly in the 1970s when the first oil crisis dramatically reduced traffic growth, interest grew in developing more varied traffic solutions. The development of integrated traffic streets started with the woonerfs in the Netherlands, but quickly spread throughout Europe. Traffic calming grew in popularity in the 1970s and quiet streets and playing streets were introduced. The new types of streets reduced traffic speed, making them considerably friendlier and safer for all types of traffic.

In recent decades, ideas about traffic reorganization and traffic integration have spread more widely around the world. The latest addition to the category of types of streets is shared streets, which function remarkably well if they are interpreted as streets on which pedestrians have a clear first priority.

Los Angeles, California

Traffic integration on the terms of fast-moving traffic. A straightforward traffic system with poor traffic safety. The streets are virtually unusable for anything but vehicular traffic.

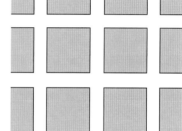

Radburn, New Jersey

Traffic separation system introduced in Radburn in 1928. A complicated, expensive system of many parallel roads and paths and many costly pedestrian tunnels. Surveys show that although in theory the system appears to improve traffic safety, it functions poorly in practice because pedestrians take the shortest route rather than the safest.

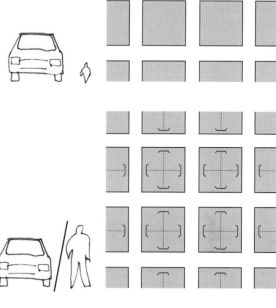

Delft, Holland

Traffic integration on the terms of slow-moving traffic, introduced in Delft in 1969. A straightforward, simple and safe system, which maintains the street as the all-important public space. When cars must be driven up to a building, traffic integration with priority for pedestrians is clearly the best system.

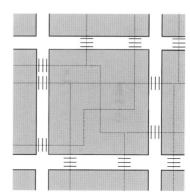

Venice, Italy

The pedestrian city, with the transition from fast to slow-moving traffic occurring at the city limits or edge of residential area. A straightforward and simple system with a considerably higher safety level and better security than any other traffic system.

Source: Jan Gehl, Life Between Buildings *(1971), 6th edition, The Danish Architectural Press, 2010. Further developed: Gehl Architects — Urban Quality Consultants, 2009.*

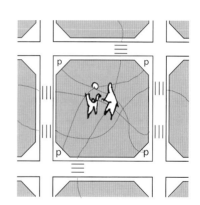

Unobstructed views, short distances, slow face-to-face movement — what more could anyone want to experience life in the city? (Sidewalk scene, Karl Johan Gate, Oslo, Norway).

To invite or repel — seeing and hearing contacts

In chapter one modest seeing and hearing contacts are highlighted as the most important and common form of contact between people in public space. Under all circumstances, seeing and hearing other people provides information, overview and inspiration. It can also be a beginning: more extensive contacts all start with seeing and hearing.

Chapter two describes how throughout the history of their development, people have been linear, frontal, horizontal, 5 km/3 mph beings. This is the starting point for the development of people's sensory apparatus and for the capacity and way our senses function. Senses also have a major impact on interaction between people, as previously described in chapter two.

With this in mind, it is simple to describe how physical planning can invite or repel basic seeing and hearing contacts.

Inviting requires unobstructed views, short distances, low speeds, staying on the same level and orientation towards what is to be experienced.

Looking closer at these prerequisites, we can see that these same physical frameworks are found in old pedestrian cities and lively pedestrian streets.

In contrast, interrupted lines of vision, large distances, high speeds, multistory placement and orientation away from people deter people from seeing and hearing others.

Looking closer at these prerequisites, we can see that these same physical frameworks are found in many new built-up areas, residential areas and suburbs.

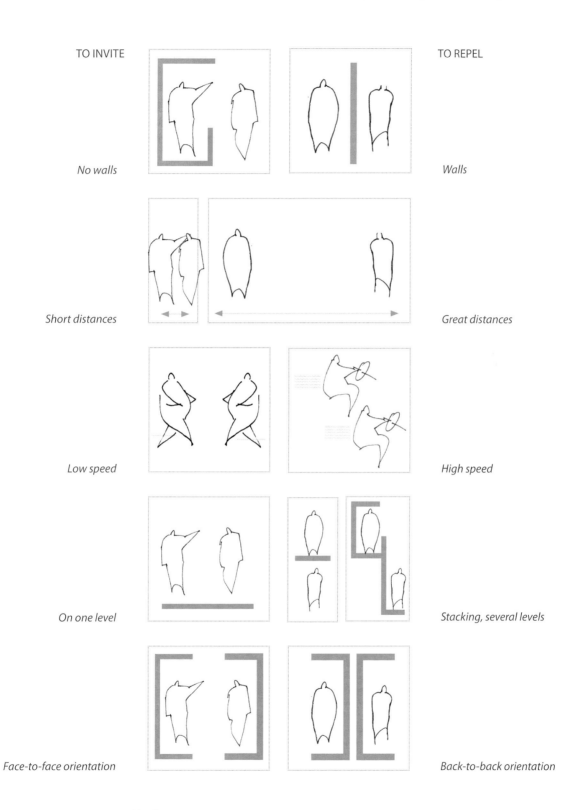

TO INVITE   TO REPEL

No walls   *Walls*

Short distances   *Great distances*

Low speed   *High speed*

On one level   *Stacking, several levels*

Face-to-face orientation   *Back-to-back orientation*

Source: Jan Gehl, Life Between Buildings *(1971), 6th edition, The Danish Architectural Press, 2010.*

If we look closer at one of the world's best functioning city space, we can see that all essential quality criteria are convincingly respected (Piazza del Campo, Siena, Italy).

The city at eye level: 12 quality criteria

The city at eye level is the theme of chapter four in which a systematic overview of the most important quality criteria is presented.

Before any other deliberations are made, it is crucial to ensure reasonable protection against risk, physical injury, insecurity and unpleasant sensory influences, the negative aspects of climate in particular. If only one of these major problems concerning protection is unmet, safeguarding the other qualities can prove meaningless.

The next step is to ensure that the spaces offer good comfort and invite people to the most important activities underlying their use of public space — walking, standing, sitting, seeing, talking, hearing and self-expression. Considerations about the situation during the day and at night as well as in the four seasons of the year are naturally part of the work to optimize city space.

Celebrating local ammenities primarily involves ensuring a good human scale, opportunities to enjoy the positive aspects of the climate in the region, as well as providing aesthetic experiences and pleasant sensory impressions. Good architecture and design are part of the twelfth and last criterion. This criterion should be seen as an umbrella concept that should include all of the other areas. It is important to emphasize that architecture and design cannot be dealt with in isolation from the other criteria.

It is interesting and thought-provoking that the finest and best functioning city spaces throughout the world demonstrates careful overall treatment of all of the quality factors mentioned. Nothing must be left out.

Protection	**PROTECTION AGAINST TRAFFIC AND ACCIDENTS — FEELING SAFE**  · Protection for pedestrians · Eliminating fear of traffic	**PROTECTION AGAINST CRIME AND VIOLENCE — FEELING SECURE** · Lively public realm · Eyes on the street · Overlapping functions day and night · Good lighting	**PROTECTION AGAINST UNPLEASANT SENSORY EXPERIENCES** · Wind · Rain/snow · Cold/heat · Pollution · Dust, noise, glare
Comfort	**OPPORTUNITIES TO WALK** · Room for walking · No obstacles · Good surfaces · Accessibility for everyone · Interesting façades	**OPPORTUNITIES TO STAND/STAY**  · Edge effect/ attractive zones for standing/staying · Supports for standing	**OPPORTUNITIES TO SIT**  · Zones for sitting · Utilizing advantages: view, sun, people · Good places to sit · Benches for resting
	OPPORTUNITIES TO SEE · Reasonable viewing distances · Unhindered sightlines · Interesting views · Lighting (when dark)	**OPPORTUNITIES TO TALK AND LISTEN** · Low noise levels · Street furniture that provides "talkscapes"	**OPPORTUNITES FOR PLAY AND EXERCISE** · Invitations for creativity, physical activity, exercise and play · By day and night · In summer and winter
Delight	**SCALE** · Buildings and spaces designed to human scale	**OPPORTUNITIES TO ENJOY THE POSITIVE ASPECTS OF CLIMATE** · Sun/shade · Heat/coolness · Breeze	**POSITIVE SENSORY EXPERIENCES** · Good design and detailing · Good materials · Fine views · Trees, plants, water

Source: Gehl, Gemzøe, Kirknæs, Søndergaard, "New City Life," The Danish Architectural Press, 2006.
Further developed: Gehl Architects — Urban Quality Consultants, 2009.

The city at eye level — designing the ground floor

The information in chapter three about strengthening life in the city emphasizes the importance of ground floors for the attractiveness and functionality of cities. This is the exchange zone between building and city, here is where life inside and outside can meet and here is where pedestrians pass close by and have time to enjoy experiences large and small on their way.

In recent decades, ground-floor design has suffered a setback in the form of large units, many closed façades, blind windows and lack of detail.

These developments have robbed many city streets of casual pedestrians, removed life from the streets and increased the feeling of insecurity once it gets dark.

With this knowledge in mind, Stockholm, Sweden, undertook a major urban renewal project in 1990 and developed a five-step scale for registering and assessing its ground floors. This made it possible to gain a broad overview of the areas and streets in the city that needed improvement (see page 81). This type of registration can be used to make comparisons between cities and districts, as well as serving as the starting point for establishing an active policy to ensure attractive ground floors along the most important city streets (see page 78).

In recent years many cities have used the methods for registering and assessing the attractiveness of ground floors as an important tool in their efforts to maintain and develop city space quality.

A — active

Small units, many doors
(15 – 20 doors per 100 m/328 feet)
Large variation in function
No blind and few passive units
Lots of character in façade relief
Primarily vertical façade articulation
Good details and materials

B — friendly

Relatively small units (10 – 14 doors per 100 m/328 feet)
Some variation in function
Few blind and passive units
Façade relief
Many details

C — mixture

Large and small units (6 – 10 doors per 100 m/328 feet)
Modest variation in function
Some blind and passive units
Modest façade relief
Few details

D — boring

Large units, few doors (2 – 5 doors per 100 m/328 feet)
Almost no variation in function
Many blind or uninteresting units
Few or no details

E — inactive

Large units, few or no doors (0 – 2 doors per 100 m/328 feet)
No visible variation in function
Blind or passive units
Uniform façades, no details, nothing to look at

Source:
"Close Encounters With Buildings," Urban Design International, 2006
Further developed: Gehl Architects — Urban Quality Consultants, 2009

 One-way streets: greater traffic capacity and more speed, but a noisy and aggressive traffic environment follow (New York City).

 ...or two-way streets with two lanes for cars, bicycle paths, trees and a median strip: a more attractive, safer street (redesigned city street in Copenhagen).

Reordering priorities, please

Over the many years in which car traffic has grown dramatically, capable traffic engineers the world over have endeavored to develop methods for increasing traffic capacity on city streets. This and the following 3 pages show ideas that ensure room for more vehicular traffic in the streets. The problem is that all of these ideas have systematically worsened the conditions for people to be able to walk in cities.

In order for city planners to incorporate the human dimension, it is necessary to reevaluate the many capacity-friendly traffic ideas that have crept their way into cities over the years. There is a good pedestrian-friendly solution to each of these problems, as shown on the following pages.

It is high time that we reorder our priorities.

Obstacles on the sidewalks
Cordoba, Argentina

...or a dignified
pedestrian experience
Riga, Latvia

Narrow sidewalks
London, UK

...or a more equal
distribution of space
Copenhagen, Denmark

Applying to cross the street
Sydney, Australia

...or being politely informed
Copenhagen, Denmark

Blinking red light urging people
to speed up while crossing
New York, USA

...or being politely informed
Copenhagen, Denmark

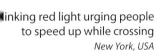

Long waits
Tokyo, Japan

...or a balance between walking and waiting
Copenhagen, Denmark

Guard rails alongside sidewalks
London, UK

...or respect for pedestrian desirelines
Kensington, London, UK

Pedestrian bridges
Nagoya, Japan

...or direct crossing at street level
Copenhagen, Denmark

Pedestrian underpasses
Zürich, Switzerland. Before

...or direct crossing at street level
Zürich, Switzerland. After

Hopping between pedestrian islands
Sydney, Australia

...or pedestrian crossings without interruptions
Copenhagen, Denmark

244   cities for people

Interruptions for minor streets
London, UK

...or sidewalks and bicycle paths taken across side streets
Copenhagen, Denmark

Sidewalks interrupted for driveways and delivery lanes
London, UK

...or sidewalks that carry on without interruptions
Copenhagen, Denmark

Confusing "slip-lanes"*Sydney, Australia*

...or simple intersections
Brisbane, Australia

Street crossings that resemble obstacle courses
London, UK

...or simple crossings
Copenhagen, Denmark

Pedestrians conducted away from street corners
Bilbao, Spain. Before

...or respect for pedestrian desire lines
Bilbao, Spain. After

Source: Gehl Architects - Urban Quality Consultants, 2009.

Notes
Bibliography
Illustrations
and photos
Index

Notes

Chapter 1

1. Jane Jacobs, *The Death and Life of Great American Cities* (New York: Random House, 1961).

2. Le Corbusier, *Propos d'urbanisme* (Paris: Éditions Bouveillier et Cie, 1946). In English: Le Corbusier, Clive Entwistle, *Concerning Town Planning* (New Haven: Yale University Press, 1948).

3. The City of New York and Mayor Michael R. Bloomberg, *Plan NYC. A Greener, Greater New York* (New York: The City of New York, 2007).

4. New York City Department of Transportation, *World Class Streets: Remaking New York City's Public Realm* (New York: New York City Department of Transportation, 2009).

5. Mayor of London, Transport for London, *Central London. Congestion Charging. Impacts Monitoring. Sixth Annual Report, July 2008* (London: Transport for London, 2008).

6. City of Copenhagen, *Copenhagen City of Cyclists — Bicycle Account 2008* (Copenhagen: City of Copenhagen, 2009).

7. Of Copenhagen residents, working or studying in the city, the cycling-share of transport is 55%: Ibid: 8.

8. Mayor of London, Transport of London, *Central London. Congestion Charging. Impacts Monitoring. Sixth Annual Report, July 2008* (London: Transport for London, 2008).

9. City of Copenhagen, *Copenhagen City of Cyclists — Bicycle Account 2008* (Copenhagen: City of Copenhagen, 2009).

10. Jan Gehl and Lars Gemzøe, *Public Spaces Public Life, Copenhagen*, 3rd ed.(Copenhagen: The Danish Architectural Press and The Royal Danish Academy of Fine Arts School of Architecture Publishers, 2004): 59.

11. Jan Gehl, Lars Gemzøe, Sia Kirknæs, Britt Sternhagen, *New City Life* (Copenhagen: The Danish Architectural Press, 2006).

12. 1968-study: Jan Gehl, "Mennesker til fods," *Arkitekten*, no. 20 (1968): 429–446. 1986-study: Karin Bergdahl, Jan Gehl, Aase Steensen, "Byliv 1986. Bylivet i Københavns indre by brugsmønstre og udviklingsmønstre 1968–1986," *Arkitekten*, special ed. no. 12 (1987); 1995-study: Jan Gehl and Lars Gemzøe, *Public Spaces Public Life, Copenhagen*, 3rd ed. (Copenhagen: The Danish Architectural Press and The Royal Danish Academy of Fine Arts School of Architecture Publishers, 2004); Jan Gehl, Lars Gemzøe, Sia Kirknæs, Britt Sternhagen, *New City Life* (Copenhagen: The Danish Ar-

chitectural Press, 2006).

[13.] City of Melbourne and Gehl Architects, *Places for People* (Melbourne: City of Melbourne, 2004).

[14.] Unpublished data from Gehl Architects.

[15.] City of Melbourne and Gehl Architects, *Places for People* (Melbourne: City of Melbourne, 2004).

[16.] Ibid.

[17.] Jan Gehl, "Public Spaces for a Changing Public Life," *Topos: European Landscape Magazine*, no. 61 (2007): 16 – 22.

[18.] Ibid.

[19.] On "life between buildings," in *Life Between Buildings*, Jan Gehl (Copenhagen: Danish Architectural Press, 1971).

[20.] The City of New York and Mayor Michael R. Bloomberg, *Plan NYC: A Greener, Greater New York* (New York: The City of New York, 2007).

[21.] Gehl Architects unpublished data.

[22.] Carolyne Larrington, trans., *The Poetic Edda* (Oxford: Oxford University Press, 1996).

[23.] Jan Gehl and Lars Gemzøe, *Public Spaces Public Life, Copenhagen*, 3rd ed. (Copenhagen: The Danish Architectural Press and The Royal Danish Academy of Fine Arts School of Architecture Publishers, 2004).

[24.] Jane Jacobs, *The Death and Life of Great American Cities* (New York: Random House, 1961).

[25.] Statistics Denmark, 2009 numbers, statistikbanken.dk.

Chapter 2

[1.] Edward T. Hall, *The Silent Language* (New York: Anchor Books/ Doubleday (1973); Edward T. Hall, *The Hidden Dimension* (Garden City, New York: Doubleday, 1990. Originally published 1966).

[2.] Edward T. Hall, *The Hidden Dimension* (Garden City, New York: Doubleday, 1990. Originally published 1966). Jan Gehl, *Life Between Buildings* (Copenhagen: Danish Architectural Press, 1971): 63–72.

[3.] Jan Gehl, *Life Between Buildings* (Copenhagen: Danish Architectural Press, 1971): 64 – 67.

[4.] Ibid.

[5.] Allan R. Tilley and Henry Dreyfuss Associates, *The Measure of Man and Woman. Human Factors in Design*, revised edition (New York: John Wiley & Sons, 2002).

[6.] Ibid.

[7.] See illustrated experiment of distances p. 40.

[8.] Jan Gehl, *Life Between Buildings* (Copenhagen: Danish Architectural Press, 1971): 69 – 72

[9.] Edward T. Hall, *The Hidden Dimension* (Garden City, New York: Doubleday, 1990).

[10.] Ibid.

Chapter 3

[1.] Approximate values based on information from Bo Grönlund, The Royal Academy of Fine Arts School of Architecture, Copenhagen.

[2.] See also Camilla Richter-Friis van Deurs, *uderum udeliv* (Copenhagen: The Royal Danish Academy of Fine Arts School of Architecture, 2010); Jan Gehl, "Soft Edges in Residential Streets," *Scandinavian Housing and Planning Research* 3 (1986): 89 – 102.

3. Jan Gehl, "Mennesker til fods," *Arkitekten*, no. 20 (1968). The numbers were tested in 2008 with comparable conclusions.

4. Jan Gehl, "Soft Edges in Residential Streets," *Scandinavian Housing and Planning Research* 3 (1986): 89 – 102.

5. Ibid.

6. Jan Gehl, "Public Spaces for a Changing Public Life," *Topos*, no. 61 (2007): 16 – 22.

7. Ibid.

8. Miloš Bobić, *Between the Edges: Street Building Transition as Urbanity Interface* (Bussum, the Netherlands: Troth Publisher Bussum, 2004).

9. Michael Varming, *Motorveje i landskabet* (Hørsholm: Statens Byggeforsknings Institut, SBi, byplanlægning, 12, 1970).

10. Jan Gehl, "Close Encounters with Buildings," *Urban Design International*, no. 1 (2006): 29 – 47. First published in Danish: Gehl, Jan, L. J. Kaefer, S. Reigstad, "Nærkontakt med huse", *Arkitekten,* no. 9 (2004): 6–21.

11. Jan Gehl, "Close Encounters with Buildings," *Urban Design International*, no. 1 (2006): 29 – 47.

12. Jan Gehl, *Public Spaces and Public Life in Central Stockholm* (Stockholm: City of Stockholm, 1990).

13. Jan Gehl, "Close Encounters with Buildings," *Urban Design International*, no. 1 (2006): 29 – 47.

14. Jan Gehl, conversation with Ralph Erskine.

15. Jan Gehl, *The Interface Between Public and Private Territories in Residential Areas* (Melbourne: Department of Architecture and Building, University of Melbourne, 1977).

16. Ibid.

17. Jan Gehl, "Soft Edges in Residential Streets," *Scandinavian Housing and Planning Research* 3 (1986): 89 – 102.

18. Camilla van Deurs, "Med udkig fra altanen: livet i boligbebyggelsernes uderum anno 2005," *Arkitekten*, no. 7 (2006): 73 – 80.

19. Aase Bundgaard, Jan Gehl and Erik Skoven, "Bløde kanter. Hvor bygning og byrum mødes," *Arkitekten*, no. 21 (1982): 421 – 438.

20. Camilla van Deurs, "Med udkig fra altanen: livet i boligbebyggelsernes uderum anno 2005," *Arkitekten*, no. 7 (2006): 73 – 80.

21. Christopher Alexander, *A Pattern Language: Towns, Buildings, Constructions* (New York: Oxford University Press, 1977): 600.

22. Camilla Damm van Deurs and Lars Gemzøe, "Gader med og uden biler," *Byplan*, no. 2 (2005): 46 – 57.

23. Jane Jacobs, *The Death and Life of Great American Cities* (New York: Random House, 1961).

24. Jan Gehl, Lars Gemzøe, Sia Kirknæs, Britt Sternhagen, *New City Life* (Copenhagen: The Danish Architectural Press, 2006): 28.

25. Ibid.

26. Bo Grönlund, "Sammenhænge mellem arkitektur og kriminalitet," *Arkitektur der forandrer*, ed. Niels Bjørn (Copenhagen: Gads Forlag, 2008): 64 – 79. Thorkild

Ærø and Gunvor Christensen, *Forebyggelse af kriminalitet i boligområder* (Hørsholm: Statens Byggeforsknings Institut, 2003).

27. Oscar Newman, *Defensible Space: Crime Prevention Through Urban Design* (New York: Macmillan, 1972).

28. Peter Newman and Jeffrey Kenworthy, *Sustainability and Cities: Overcomming Automobile Dependency* (Washington, D.C.: Island Press, 1999).

29. Peter Newman, Timothy Beatley, Heather Boyer, *Resilient Cities: Responding to Peak Oil and Climate Change* (Washington DC: Island Press, 2009).

30. City of Copenhagen, *Copenhagen City of Cyclists – Bicycle Account 2008* (Copenhagen: City of Copenhagen, 2009).

31. Illustrations based on accumulated numbers from 2000 – 2007. World Health Organization, *World Health Statistics 2009* (France: World Health Organization, 2009).

32. World Health Organization, *World Health Statistics 2009* (France: World Health Organization, 2009).

33. Centers for Disease Control and Prevention: www.cdc.gov/Features/ChildhoodObesity (accessed January 21, 2009).

34. World Health Organization, *World Health Statistics 2009* (France: World Health Organization, 2009).

35. Chanam Lee and Anne Vernez Moudon, "Neighbourhood Design and Physical Activity," *Building Research & Information* (London: Routledge 36:5, 2008): 395 – 411.

Chapter 4

1. Jan Gehl, "Mennesker til fods," *Arkitekten*, no. 20 (1968): 429-446. Walking speed on Strøget tested in 2008 with comparable results.

2. Peter Bosselmann, *Representation of Places: Reality and Realism in City Design* (Berkelcy, CA: University of California Press, 1998).

3. Gehl Architects, *Towards a Fine City for People: Public Spaces and Public Life – London 2004* (London: Transport for London, 2004); New York City Department of Transportation, *World Class Streets: Remaking New York City's Public Realm* (New York: New York City Department of Transportation, 2008); Gehl Architects, *Public Spaces, Public Life. Sydney 2007* (Sydney: City of Sydney, 2007).

4. William H. Whyte, pps.org/info/placemakingtools/placemakers/wwhyte (accessed February 8, 2010); John J. Fruin, *Designing for Pedestrians: A level of service concept* (Department of Transportation, Planning and Engineering, Polytechnic Institute of Brooklyn, 1970): 51.

5. Gehl Architects, *Towards a Fine City for People. Public Spaces and Public Life — London 2004* (London: Transport for London, 2004).

6. Gehl Architects, *Public Spaces and Public Life. City of Adelaide 2002* (Adelaide: City of Adelaide, 2002).

7. Gehl Architects, *Public Spaces, Public Life. Sydney 2007* (Sydney: City of Sydney, 2007).

8. Jan Gehl, "Mennesker til fods," *Arkitekten*, no. 20 (1968): 429-446.

Tested in 2008 with comparable conclusions.

9. Jan Gehl, *Public Space. Public Life in Central Stockholm 1990* (Stockholm: City of Stockholm, 1990).

10. Jan Gehl, *Stadsrum & stadsliv i Stockholms city* (Stockholm: Stockholms Fastighetskontor and Stockholms Stadsbyggnadskontor, 1990).

11. William H. Whyte, *The Social Life of Small Urban Spaces*, film produced by The Municipal Art Society (New York 1990).

12. Jan Gehl, "Soft edges in residential streets," *Scandinavian Housing and Planning Research* 3, (1986): 89 – 102; Jan Gehl, *Stadsrum & Stadsliv i Stockholms City* (Stockholm: Stockholms Fastighetskontor. Stockholms Stadsbyggnadskontor, 1991). Jan Gehl, "Close encounters with buildings," *Urban Design International*, no. 1 (2006): 29–47; Camilla van Deurs, "Med udkig fra altanen: livet i boligbebyggelsernes uderum anno 2005," *Arkitekten*, no. 7 (2006): 73 – 80.

13. Philadelphia data: unpublished data, Gehl Arhcitects. *Perth data: Gehl Architects, Perth 2009. Public Spaces & Public Life* (Perth: City of Perth, 2009): 47. Stockholm data: unpublished data, Gehl Architects. Copenhagen data: Jan Gehl, Lars Gemzøe, Sia Kirknæs, Britt Sternhagen, *New City Life*, (Copenhagen: The Danish Architetural Press, 2006): 41; Melbourne data 1993, 2004: City of Melbourne and Gehl Architects, *Places for People. Melbourne 2004* (Melbourne: City of Melbourne, 2004): 32. 2009 numbers from Parks and Urban Design, City of Melbourne.

14. Jan Gehl, Lars Gemzøe, Sia Kirknæs, Britt Sternhagen, *New City Life* (Copenhagen: The Danish Architectural Press 2006). City of Melbourne and Gehl Architects, *Places for People*. Melbourne 2004 (Melbourne: City of Melbourne, 2004).

15. Joseph A. Salvato, Nelson L. Nemerow og Franklin J. Agardy, eds. *Environmental Engineering*, (Hoboken, New Jersey: John Wiley and Sons, 2003).

16. Jan Gehl et al., "Studier i Burano," *Arkitekten*, no. 18 (1978).

17. Gehl Architects (London 2004): Gehl Architects (Sydney 2007) New York City Department of Transportation (2008)

18. Camillo Sitte, *The Art of Building Cities* (Westport, Conneticut: Hyperion Press reprint 1979 of 1945 version). Originally published in German: Camillo Sitte, *Der Städtebau — künstlerischen Grundsätzen* (Wien: Verlag von Carl Graeser, 1889).

19. Peter Bosselmann et al., *Sun, Wind, and Comfort: A Study of Open Spaces and Sidewalks in Four Downtown Areas* (Environmental Simulation Laboratory, Institute of Urban and Regional Development, College of Environmental Design, University of California, Berkeley, 1984): 19 – 23.

20. Inger Skjervold Rosenfeld, "Klima og boligområder," *Landskap*, vol. 57, no. 2 (1976): 28– 31.

21. Peter Bosselmann, *The Coldest Winter I Ever Spent: The Fight for Sunlight in San Francisco* documentary film produced by Peter Bosselmann, 1997.

22. On the case of San Francisco,

see: Peter Bosselmann et al., *Sun, Wind, and Comfort: A Study of Open Spaces and Sidewalks in Four Downtown Areas* (Environmental Simulation Laboratory, Institute of Urban and Regional Development, College of Environmental Design, University of California, Berkeley, 1984). Peter Bosselmann, *Urban Transformation* (Washington DC: Island Press, 2008).

23. William H. Whyte, *City: Rediscovering the Center* (New York: Doubleday, 1988).

24. The City of New York and Mayor Michael R. Bloomberg, *Plan NYC: A Greener, Greater New York* (New York: The City of New York, 2007).

25. Numbers provided by City of Copenhagen.

26. City of Copenhagen, *Copenhagen City of Cyclists – Bicycle Account 2006* (Copenhagen: City of Copenhagen, 2006).

27. Eric Britton and Associates, *Vélib. City Bike Strategies. A New Mobility Advisory Brief* (Paris: Eric Britton and Associates, 2007).

Chapter 5

1. Public space public life studies, Copenhagen: 1968: Jan Gehl, "Mennesker til fods," *Arkitekten*, no. 20 (1968): 429 – 446; 1986-study: Karin Bergdahl, Jan Gehl & Aase Steensen, "Byliv 1986. Bylivet i Københavns indre by brugsmønstre og udviklingsmønstre 1968–1986," *Arkitekten*, special ed. (1987); 1995-study: Jan Gehl and Lars Gemzøe, *Public Spaces – Public Life*, 3rd ed. (Copenhagen, The Danish Architectural Press and The Royal Danish Academy of Fine Arts School of Architecture Publishers2004); 2005-study: Jan Gehl, Lars Gemzøe, Sia Kirknæs, Britt Sternhagen, *New City Life* (Copenhagen: The Danish Architectural Press, 2006).

2. Data in illustration from: Gehl Architects, *City to waterfront — Wellington October 2004. Public Spaces and Public Life Study* (Wellington: City of Wellington, 2004). Gehl Architects, Downtown Seattle Public Space & Public Life (Seattle: International Sustainability Institute, 2009); Gehl Architects, *Public Spaces, Public Life. Sydney 2007* (Sydney: City of Sydney, 2007). Gehl Architects, Stockholmsförsöket och stadslivet i Stockholms innerstad (Stockholm: City of Stockholm, 2006); Gehl Architects, *Public Spaces, Public Life. Perth 2009* (Perth: City of Perth, 2009). New York City, Department of Transportation (DOT), *World Class Streets* (New York: DOT, 2009); Gehl Architects, *Towards a Fine City for People. Public Spaces and Public Life — London 2004* (London: Transport for London 2004); City of Melbourne and Gehl Architects, *Places for People. Melbourne 2004* (City of Melbourne, 2004); Jan Gehl, Lars Gemzøe, Sia Kirknæs, Britt Sternhagen, *New City Life* (Copenhagen: The Danish Architectural Press, 2006).

3. Several of the projects can be downloaded at www.gehlarchitects.dk

4. Jan Gehl and Lars Gemzøe, *Public Spaces Public Life, Copenhagen*, 3rd ed. (Copenhagen: The Danish Architectural Press and The Ro-

yal Danish Academy of Fine Arts School of Architecture Publishers, 2004): 62.

Chapter 6

1. *The Endless City : The Urban Age Project by the London School of Economics and Deutsche Bank's Alfred Herrhausen Society*, eds. Ricky Burdett and Deyan Sudjic (London: Phaidon, 2007): 9.

2. Population Division of Economic and Social Affairs, United Nations Secretariat, "The World of Six Billion," United Nations 1999, p. 8. www.un.org/esa/population/publications/sixbillion/sixbilpart1.pdf.

3. ibid.

4. *The Endless City : The Urban Age Project by the London School of Economics and Deutsche Bank's Alfred Herrhausen Society,* eds. Ricky Burdett and Deyan Sudjic (London: Phaidon, 2007): 9.

5. Mahabubul Bari and Debra Efroymson, *Dhaka Urban transport project's after project report: a critical review* (Dhaka: Roads for People, WBB Trust, April 2006). Mahabubul Bari and Debra Efroymson, *Improving Dhaka's Traffic Situation: Lessons from Mirpur Road* (Dhaka: Roads for People, February 2005).

6. Enrique Peñalosa, "A dramatic Change towards a People City — the Bogota Story," keynote address presented at the conference *Walk 21 — V Cities For People*, June 9 – 11, 2004, Copenhagen, Denmark.

7. Barbara Southworth, "Urban Design in Action: The City of Cape Town's Dignified Places Programme — Implementation of New Public Spaces towards Integration and Urban Regeneration in South Africa," *Urban Design International*, no. 8 (2002): 119 – 133.

8. Unpublished interview with Ralph Erskine as part of the documentary: Lars Oxfeldt Mortensen, *Cities for People, a nordic coproduction* DR, SR, NRK, RUV, YLE 2000.

Bibliography

Alexander, Christopher. *A Pattern Language: Towns, Buildings, Constructions.* New York: Oxford University Press, 1977.

Bari, Mahabubul, and Debra Efroymson. *Dhaka Urban Transport Projects. After project report: A critical review.* Roads for People, WBB Trust, April 2006.

Bari, Mahabubul, and Debra Efroymson. *Improving Dhaka's Traffic Situation: Lessons from Mirpur Road.* Dhaka: Roads for People, February, 2005.

Bobić, Miloš. *Between the Edges: Street Building Transition as Urbanity Interface.* Bussum, the Netherlands: Troth Publisher Bussum, 2004.

Bosselmann, Peter. *The coldest winter I ever spent: The fight for sunlight in San Francisco,* (documentary), producer: Peter Bosselmann, 1997.

Bosselmann, Peter. *Representation of Places: Reality and Realism in City Design.* Berkeley, CA: University of California Press, 1998.

Bosselmann, Peter et al. *Sun, Wind, and Comfort: A Study of Open Spaces and Sidewalks in Four Downtown Areas.* Environmental Simulation Laboratory, Institute of Urban and Regional Development, College of Environmental Design, University of California, Berkeley, 1984.

Bosselmann, Peter. *Urban Transformation.* Washington DC: Island Press, 2008.

Britton, Eric and Associates. *Vélib. City bike strategies. A new mobility advisory brief.* Paris: Eric Britton and Associates, November, 2007.

Burdett, Ricky and Deyan Sudjic, eds. *The Endless City: The Urban Age Project by the London School of Economics and Deutsche Bank's Alfred Herrhausen Society,* London: Phaidon, 2007.

Centers for Disease Control and Prevention: www.cdc.gov/Features/Childhood Obesity (accessed January 21, 2009).

City of Copenhagen. *Bicycle account 2006.* Copenhagen: City of Copenhagen, 2006.

City of Copenhagen. *Copenhagen city of cyclists — Bicycle account 2008.* Copenhagen: City of Copenhagen, 2009.

City of Melbourne and Gehl Architects. *Places for People. Melbourne 2004.* Melbourne: City of Melbourne, *2004.*

The City of New York and Mayor Michael R. Bloomberg. *Plan NYC: A Greener, Greater New York.* New York: The City of New York and Mayor Michael R. Bloomberg, 2007.

Fruin, John J. *Designing for pedestrians. A level of service concept.* Department of Transportation, Planning and Engineering, Polytechnic Institute of Brooklyn, 1970.

Gehl Architects: www.gehlarchitects.dk.

Gehl Architects. *City to waterfront — Wellington October 2004. Public spaces and public life study.* Wellington: City of Wellington, 2004.

Gehl Architects. *Downtown Seattle public space & public life.* Seattle: International Sustainability Institute, 2009.

Gehl Architects. *Perth 2009. Public spaces & public life.* Perth: City of Perth, 2009.

Gehl Architects. *Public spaces and public life. City of Adelaide 2002.* Adelaide: City of Adelaide, 2002.

Gehl Architects. *Public spaces, public life. Sydney 2007.* Sydney: City of Sydney, 2007.

Gehl Architects. *Stockholmsförsöket och stadslivet i Stockholms innerstad.* Stockholm: Stockholm Stad, 2006.

Gehl Architects. *Towards a fine city for people. Public spaces and public life — London 2004.* London: Transport for London, 2004.

Gehl, Jan. *Close encounters with buildings.* Urban Design international, no. 1, (2006): 29 – 47. First published in Danish: Gehl, Jan, L. J. Kaefer, S. Reigstad. "Nærkontakt med huse." *Arkitekten,* no. 9, (2004): 6 – 21.

Gehl, Jan. *Life Between Buildings.* Danish Architecture Press, 1971. Distributed by Island Press.

Gehl, Jan. "Mennesker til fods." *Arkitekten,* no. 20 (1968): 429– 446.

Gehl, Jan. *The interface between public and private territories in residential areas*. Melbourne: Department of Architecture and Building, University of Melbourne, 1977.

Gehl, Jan. *Public Spaces and public life in central Stockholm*. Stockholm: City of Stockholm, 1990.

Gehl, Jan. "Public spaces for a changing public life." *Topos: European Landscape Magazine*, no. 61, (2007): 16 – 22.

Gehl, Jan. "Soft edges in residential streets." Scandinavian Housing and Planning Research 3, (1986): 89 – 102.

Gehl, Jan, Aa. Bundgaard, and E. Skoven. "Bløde kanter. Hvor bygning og byrum mødes." *Arkitekten*, no. 21, (1982): 421 – 438.

Gehl, Jan et al. "Studier i Burano." special ed. *Arkitekten*, no. 18, (1978).

Gehl, Jan, K. Bergdahl, and Aa. Steensen. "Byliv 1986. Bylivet i Københavns indre by brugsmønstre og udviklingsmønstre 1968 - 1986." *Arkitekten*, special print, Copenhagen: 1987.

Gehl, Jan, L. Gemzøe, S. Kirknæs, and B. Sternhagen. *New City Life*. Copenhagen: Danish Architectural Press, 2006.

Gehl, Jan, and L. Gemzøe. *Public Spaces Public Life Copenhagen*. 3rd ed. Copenhagen: Danish Architectural Press and The Royal Danish Academy of Fine Arts School of Architecture Publishers, 2004.

Grönlund, Bo. "Sammenhænge mellem arkitektur og kriminalitet." Arkitektur der forandrer, ed. Niels Bjørn, Copenhagen: Gads Forlag, 2008: 64 – 79.

Hall, Edward T. *The Silent Language*. New York: Anchor Books/Doubleday, 1973.

Hall, Edward T. *The Hidden Dimension*. Garden City, New York: Doubleday, 1990. Originally published 1966.

Jacobs, Jane. *The Death and Life of Great American Cities*. New York: Random House, 1961.

Larrington, Carolyne, trans., *The Poetic Edda*. Oxford: Oxford University Press, 1996.

Le Corbusier. *Propos d'urbanisme*. Paris: Éditions Bouveillier et Cie., 1946. In English: Le Corbusier, Clive Entwistle, *Concerning town planning*. New Haven:

Yale University Press, 1948.

Mayor of London, Transport for London. *Central London. Congestion Charging. Impacts Monitoring. Sixth Annual Report, July 2008.* London: Transport for London, 2008.

Mortensen, Lars O. Livet mellem husene/Life between buildings, documentary, nordic coproduction DR, SR, NRK, RUV, YLE, 2000.

Moudon, Anne Vernez, and Lee Chanam. "Neighbourhood design and physical activity." Building Research & Information 36(5), Routledge, London (2008): 395 – 411.

Newman, Oscar. *Defensible Space: Crime Prevention Through Urban Design.* New York: Macmillan, 1972.

Newman, Peter, T. Beatley, and H. Boyer. *Resilient Cities: Responding to Peak Oil and Climate Change.* Washington DC: Island Press, 2009.

Newman, Peter, and Jeffrey Kenworthy. Sustainability and Cities: Overcoming Automobile Dependency. Washington: Island Press, 1999.

New York City Department of Transportation. *World class streets: Remaking New York City's public realm.* New York: New York City Department of Transportation, 2008.

Peñalosa, Enrique. "A dramatic change towards a people city — the Bogota story," keynote address presented at the conference *Walk 21 — V Cities for people*, June 9 – 11, 2004, Copenhagen, Denmark.

Population Division of Economic and Social Affairs. United Nations Secretariat: "The World of Six Billion," United Nations (1999) www.un.org/esa/population/publications/sixbillion/sixbilpart1.pdf.

Rosenfeld, Inger Skjervold. "Klima og boligområder." *Landskap*, Vol. 57, no. 2, (1976): 28 – 31.

Salvato, Joseph A., Nelson L. Nemerow, and Franklin J. Agardy, eds. *Environmental Engineering*, Hoboken, New Jersey: John Wiley & Sons, 2003.

Sitte, Camillo. *The Art of Building Cities.* Westport, Conneticut: Hyperion Press, reprint 1979 of 1945 version. First published in German: Camillo Sitte. *Der Städtebau — künstlerischen Grundsätzen.* Wien: Verlag von Carl Graeser, 1889.

Sourthworth, Barbara. "Urban design in action: The city of Cape Town's dignified places programme — implementation of new public spaces towards integration and urban regeneration in South Africa." *Urban Design International* 8, (2002): 119 – 133.

Statistics Denmark, 2009 numbers, statistikbanken.dk.

Tilley, A.R. and Henry Dreyfuss Associates. *The Measure of Man and Woman. Human Factors in Design*. revised edition. New York: John Wiley & Sons, 2002.

van Deurs, Camilla Damm. "Med udkig fra altanen: livet i boligbebyggelsernes uderum anno 2005." *Arkitekten*, no. 7 (2006): 73 – 80.

van Deurs, Camilla Damm, and Lars Gemzøe. "Gader med og uden biler." Byplan, no. 2 (2005): 4 – 57.

van Deurs, Camilla Richter-Friis. *uderum udeliv*. Copenhagen: The Royal Danish Academy of Fine Arts School of Architecture Publishers (2010).

Varming, Michael. Motorveje i landskabet. Hørsholm: Statens Byggeforsknings Institut, SBi, byplanlægning, 12, 1970.

Whyte, William H. City: *Rediscovering the Center*. New York: Doubleday, 1988.

Whyte, William H. "The Social Life of Small Urban Spaces." Film produced by The Municipal Art Society of New York, 1990.

Whyte, William H. quoted from web site of Project for Public Spaces: pps.org/info/placemakingtools/placemakers/wwhyte (accessed February 2, 2010).

World Health Organization. *World Health Statistics 2009*. France: World Health Organization, 2009.

Ærø, Thorkild, and G. Christensen. *Forebyggelse af kriminalitet i boligområder*. Hørsholm: Statens Byggeforsknings Institut, 2003.

Illustrations and photos

Illustrations

Le Corbusier, *p.4*
(c) 2010 Artists Rights Society (ARS),
New York / ADAGP, Paris / F.L.C.
Camilla Richter-Friis van Deurs,
remaining illustrations

Photos

Tore Brantenberg, p. 64 middle,
p. 131 above
Adam Brandstrup, p. 110 middle
Byarkitektur, Århus Kommune, p.
16 above left
Birgit Cold, p. 32 middle
City of Malmö, p. 201 above right
City of Melbourne, p. 178 above
middle, above right, below left and
right, p. 179, below left.
City of Sydney, p. 98 above right.
**Department of Transportation, New
York City**, p. 11 below, left and right,
p. 190
Hans H. Johansen, p. 208 middle
Troels Heien, p. 10 middle
Neil Hrushowy, p. 8 middle
Brynjólfur Jónsson, p. 51 below
HafenCity, chapter 5 start.
Heather Josten, p. 208 below
Peter Schulz Jørgensen, p. 28 above
left

Jesper Kirknæs, p. 212 – 213.
Gösta Knudsen, p. 16 above right
Daniel Kukla, p. V
Paul Moen, p. 69 below right
Kian Ang Onn, p. 54 above right
Naja Rosing-Asvid, p. 160 middle
Paul Patterson, p. 98 above right
Project for Public Spaces, p. 17 below
Solvejg Reigstad, p. 154 below, p.
166 below
Jens Rørbech, p. 12 above left, p. 22
above left
Ole Smith, p. 100 above left
Shaw and Shaw, p. 15 below left and
right
Barbara Southworth, p. 225, p. 226
above right
Michael Varming, p. 206 above left
Bjarne Vinterberg, p. 92 above

Jan Gehl and **Gehl Architects**,
remaining photos

Index

Figures/photos/illustrations are indicated by a "f."

from tall buildings, 42
community workshops, 50–51
commuting, 10f, 106f, 107, 182
concentrating activities, 65
confidence, 29
Copenhagen, Denmark, 11–12, 12f, 13,
29, 64f, 71, 73f, 102f, 120, 125, 127f, 129,
150f, 164f, 166f, 197, 207, 243, 244, 245
   activity patterns in, 85
   bicycle accidents, 186f
   bicycle lanes, 124f
   bicycle share system in, 187
   bicycling in, 10f, 11, 107, 113, 182
   car traffic in, 10f
   city center, 121f
   city life studies, 72–73, 209–211
   commercial/cultural activities in,
211f
   commuting in, 10f, 107, 182
   density, 69
   ground floors problem registration in, 81f
   inviting people v. cars in, 13
   light in, 98f, 99
   monitoring city life in, 13
   neighborhoods from aerial view,
206–207
   noise levels in, 153
   pedestrian priority streets in, 12f, 13
   public transportation in, 184f
   redesigned streets in, 242f
   row houses, 206f
   seating in, 143f, 211f
   shrinking households in, 27–28
   sidewalk cafés in, 146f, 175f
   staying activities in, 12f
   walking in, 12f, 13, 21, 113, 120, 125,
129
   wind in, 170f
Cordoba, Argentina, 243
Cordoba, Spain, 142
Costa, Lúcio da, 196
Curitiba, Brazil, 220–221

D

The Death and Life of Great American
Cities (Jacobs), 3, 97
Dead Sea, 59f
defensible space, 102
Delft, Netherlands, 235
density
   in Aker Brygge, Oslo, Norway, 69
   compact, 73
   Copenhagen, Denmark, 69
   liveliness and, 68–69
   in new urban areas, 69
   New York City, 68
   in old cities, 69
   Paris, France, 69
   street life and, 83
   Sydney, Australia, 68
   tall buildings and, 68
developing countries
   bicycling in, 190–191, 217–218
   common features of, 219
   housing problems, 215, 217
   outdoor activities in, 216f, 219
   overpopulation, 215, 217
   staying activities in, 135f
Dhaka, Bangladesh, 190–191, 216f, 218f
dispersion planning principles,
232–233
distance
   age and, 34
   arm's length, 48f, 49–50, 155
   body language and, 34
   communication, 47, 101
   dominant emotions and, 34
   facial expression and, 34, 37f
   gender and, 34
   hearing, 34–35
   impressions and, 47
   intimate, 46f, 47
   language and, 48–49
   movement and, 34
   perception and, 33–35, 127
   personal, 46f, 47
   physical, 127

   public, 46f, 47–48
   senses, 33
   social, 46f, 47
   walking, 67, 121, 126f, 127f, 129
Dublin, Ireland, 41f

E

edges, 79, 103, 137
   in Bogota, Colombia, 86f
   in Cape Town, 86f
   city space without, 137
   defining space, 75
   details and, 78f
   examples, 74f, 136f
   as exchange zone, 75
   as experience zone, 76–77
   failure, 88
   in Frederiksberg, Denmark, 100f
   liveliness and, 74–88
   mixed functions and, 78f
   in Montreal, 86f
   in New Orleans, 86f
   in Norwegian housing, 85f
   reinforcing city life, 88
   in residential areas, 82
   rhythm and, 78f
   safety and, 99
   scale and, 78f
   senses and, 78f, 137
   social contact norms and, 137
   as staying zone, 75–76
   street life and, 82–85
   in Sydney, Australia, 86f
   texture and, 78f
   in Tokyo, 86f
   transparency and, 78f
   in various cultural contexts, 87
   walking and, 77, 79
elevators, 49
energy consumption, 104f, 105, 126
Erskine, Ralph, 57, 82, 150f, 155, 200,
201, 229

perception, 33–35, 43, 127

Perth, Australia, 52f, 146f, 211f

Philadelphia, Pennsylvania, 146f, 199

piano effect, 137–139

Piazza del Campo, Siena, Italy, 38, 139, 160f, 163, 165, 177, 238f

Pittsburgh, Pennsylvania, 121f

planned common activities, 23

playground
    built-in, 159f
    modernism and, 158
    Venice, Italy as, 158

population
    in developing countries, 215, 217
    historical, 66
    world, 214f, 215

Portland, Oregon, 9, 176f

Portofino, Italy, 32, 162–163

poverty, 215

proportions, 162–167

public space, ix, 3, 6
    as forum for exchange of ideas/ opinions, 28
    strengthening, 28

public transportation, 7
    bicycles in combination with, 109, 184f
    in Copenhagen, Denmark, 184f
    in London, England, 11
    prerequisites for good, 107
    in Venice, Italy, 107
    walking in combination with, 109

Q

quality criteria, 238–239

R

Radburn, New Jersey, 235

ramps, 130f, 131

registering life, 209

respect, 58f, 229

Reykjavik, Iceland, 51f, 147f, 168f

Riga, Latvia, 243

rock concerts, 36

Roman Empire, 9

Rome, Italy, 42f, 131, 131f, 134–135, 163

Rotterdam, Netherlands, 173

running, 43, 110f, 113

S

safety, 6, 91–103
    bicycle, 90f, 185, 189
    clear structures and, 101
    ground floor designs and, 99
    housing and, 99
    light and, 98
    ordinary concern and, 101
    presence of others and, 98–99
    public space for, strengthening, 28
    security and, 97–103
    society and, 97
    soft edges and, 99
    street, 19
    territories and, 101–103
    traffic, 91–95
    walking and, 6

St. Pölten, Austria, 166f, 180

San Francisco, California, 8f, 9, 173–174, 177, 182

San José, Costa Rica, 106f

Sandviken, Sweden, 200

Santiago Atitlán, Guatemala, 56f

Savannah, Georgia, 199–200

scale, 162–167
    afterwards, 167
    architecture and, 164
    building technology and, 56
    city, 195, 196
    climate and, 174
    confusion in Venice, Italy, 54f
    coordinating, 195

development, 196
    edges and, 78f
    Eurolille, Lille, France and, 166f
    large, 53f, 56
    Ørestad, Copenhagen and, 166f
    quality of, 163–164
    rapid, 164
    relations and cars, 54f
    St. Pölten, Austria and, 166f
    senses and, 33–46
    shattered, 54–59, 167
    shift in Singapore, 54f
    site planning, 195
    slow, 164
    small spaces in larger ones, 165
    speed and, 44f
    temperature and, 52f, 53f
    traditional knowledge about, 55
    in Vancouver, 203

scale, small, 207f
    invitations and, 207
    quality and, 118
    warmth and, 52f, 53f

seating, 140. See also city furniture; sidewalk cafés
    in Aker Brygge, Oslo, 17f
    arena, 37–38
    attractive, 140–141
    in Copenhagen, 143f, 211f
    design, 142f
    in HafenCity, Hamburg, 143f
    in Hasselt, Belgium, 144f
    location, 142f
    moveable, 144–145, 166f
    primary, 141–143, 144
    secondary, 141–143
    in Stockholm, Sweden, 140, 141
    in Sydney, Australia, 143f
    variation in, 141
    in Venice, Italy, 143
    waiting time, 141

sedentary work, 111

seeing activities, 23, 148, 236–237

self-expression, 158–161

Washington D.C., 170f
weather. See also climate
bicycling and, 182
   building despite, 173
   building with, 171–172
   comfortable, 169–171
   at eye level, 168–175
   liveliness and, 71
   optional activities and, 20
   preoccupation with, 168
   in Reykjavik, Iceland, 168f
   San Francisco and, 173–174
   Scandinavian, 169–172
   walking and, 120
Whyte, William H., 123, 143, 177
wind, 169–173, 170f

Y

Yogyakarta, Indonesia, 135f

Z

Zanzibar, Tanzania, 32, 216f
Zürich, Switzerland, 121f, 133f, 244

About Island Press

Since 1984, the nonprofit Island Press has been stimulating, shaping, and communicating the ideas that are essential for solving environmental problems worldwide. With more than 800 titles in print and some 40 new releases each year, we are the nation's leading publisher on environmental issues. We identify innovative thinkers and emerging trends in the environmental field. We work with world-renowned experts and authors to develop cross-disciplinary solutions to environmental challenges.

Island Press designs and implements coordinated book publication campaigns in order to communicate our critical messages in print, in person, and online using the latest technologies, programs, and the media. Our goal: to reach targeted audiences—scientists, policymakers, environmental advocates, the media, and concerned citizens—who can and will take action to protect the plants and animals that enrich our world, the ecosystems we need to survive, the water we drink, and the air we breathe.

Island Press gratefully acknowledges the support of its work by the Agua Fund, Inc., The Margaret A. Cargill Foundation, Betsy and Jesse Fink Foundation, Furthermore: a program of the J. M. Kaplan Fund, The William and Flora Hewlett Foundation, The Kresge Foundation, The Forrest and Frances Lattner Foundation, The Andrew W. Mellon Foundation, The Curtis and Edith Munson Foundation, The Overbrook Foundation, The David and Lucile Packard Foundation, The Summit Foundation, Trust for Architectural Easements, The Winslow Foundation, and other generous donors.

The opinions expressed in this book are those of the author(s) and do not necessarily reflect the views of our donors.